TAKING IT FROM BEHIND

TAKING IT
FROM BEHIND

From Boycott to Blewett:
Cricket's Changing Face in
Yorkshire's Quest for Glory

RICHARD BLAKEY

with ANDREW COLLOMOSSE

MAINSTREAM
PUBLISHING

EDINBURGH AND LONDON

First published in Great Britain in 1999 by
MAINSTREAM PUBLISHING COMPANY (EDINBURGH) LTD
7 Albany Street
Edinburgh EH1 3UG

ISBN 1 84018 240 7

A catalogue record for this book is available from the British Library

Typeset in Berkeley Book and Gill Sans
Printed and bound in Great Britain by Butler and Tanner

To so many team-mates who have made my cricket career so much fun, to Mum and Dad for their dedicated support and, above all, to my boys, Harrison and Ashton.

ACKNOWLEDGEMENTS

Many people have helped me with my book. I thank you all. And I would like to say a special thanks to the sports staff at the *Huddersfield Daily Examiner* for their help with pictures and all their support throughout my career. Also to everyone at Yorkshire County Cricket Club. And to Geoff Hughes, of Rawholme Ltd, Professional Computer Consultants, Hebden Bridge, West Yorkshire . . . for his experience.

FOREWORD

Bonjour, mon ami Blakes. Comment ça va?

So who said all fast bowlers are thick? Mind you, that's about as far as I go with the French . . . but even that basic knowledge of the language is one of many things I owe Dick Blakey.

I used to travel with Dick when I first made it into the Yorkshire side around ten years ago. And you can imagine it was a bit of a culture shock to a young lad from Barnsley when he insisted on playing French language tapes instead of some decent music.

As I was only a kid, I just had to grin and bear it at first. But in the end, I decided enough was enough and demanded a change.

I got one. Dick appeared for our next trip with an *I-Spy Guide to British Trees*, telling me to keep him informed about the various different species we encountered on our journey.

There isn't much scope for tree-spotting on the M1, though. So in the end, Dick gave up and the music started. But I hear the French tapes have been resurrected this year for the benefit of Chris Silverwood.

Blakes is quite a character. He's one of the quieter men in the dressing-room but he's never far away when there's a good prank to be played. And he's always great value on the social side.

But the bottom line as far as I'm concerned is that he's one of the top three or four wicketkeepers in the country.

He's been at the other end of the wicket for just about every ball I have bowled for Yorkshire and has played a major role in my development as an international cricketer.

In ten seasons, I can count on one hand the number of chances he's spilled off my bowling. And you cannot begin to believe how important it is to know that if you find the edge, the keeper is going to catch it, 999 times out of 1,000.

His quiet advice, encouragement and tactical know-how have also been a tremendous help to me down the years. His knowledge of the game and ability to spot a player's weakness are second to none.

He should have played far more times for England but he was so unlucky that his only tour was that nightmare trip to India seven years ago. And it's typical of Blakes that he agreed to become Yorkshire's wicketkeeper at a time when he was on the brink of an England place as a specialist batsman.

It's taken us all by surprise to learn that he's writing a book and I'm reliably informed that there's some good-natured stick about D. Gough in the ensuing pages.

Coming from Dick Blakey, I've no complaints about that. *C'est la vie*, as they say.

Darren Gough
November 1999

YORKSHIRE V GLOUCESTERSHIRE, HEADINGLEY

Tuesday, 20 April. The Indoor School, Headingley. Yorkshire's pre-season photocall moves inside as heavy rain threatens to disrupt the first game of the 1999 Championship season against Gloucestershire tomorrow. World Cup players Darren Gough and Gavin Hamilton, overseas man Greg Blewett, England A skipper Michael Vaughan and Yorkshire captain David Byas take centre-stage aided and abetted by sponsors' teapots, aprons and, to the delight of Gough and Vaughan, cream-topped fruit pies. Proceedings degenerate into slapstick. Tomorrow, though, it gets serious as Yorkshire open the campaign for their first County Championship success for a generation.

What a day! Wet, cold, grey and horrible. Is it any wonder that, as a new cricket season dawns, football remains the centre of the sporting world's attention? County Championship cricket barely merits a mention in most of the national press – apart from last week's pictures of The Riverside Ground at Chester-le-Street covered in snow. Manchester United's pursuit of a Championship, FA Cup and European Cup treble hog the back pages. As a lifelong Leeds United fan, I'm not impressed.

What does strike a chord, though, is that it's 31 years since Manchester won the European Cup for the first and, so far, only time. And that just happens to be the year when Yorkshire won the last of their 29 County Championships. For a club that, historically speaking, could reasonably claim to be the Manchester United of English cricket, that's a hell of a long wait.

I was only 19 months old when Brian Close's team won the title back in 1968 so please forgive me if my memories are a bit hazy. But since 1985 I have been a regular member of the Yorkshire team; longer than anyone else currently in the squad.

When I started, Geoffrey Boycott was opening the batting. I've seen Yorkshire open the door to overseas players and White Rose legends like David Bairstow, Phil Carrick, Arnie Sidebottom and Martyn Moxon slip away from the first-class game. All without a Championship medal.

So you will appreciate that Alex Ferguson's Holy Grail at Manchester United is not top of my priority list at the moment. Here in Yorkshire, we have our dreams, too. Last year we came closer to winning the title than at any time since I've been involved, finishing third after winning our last five games on the bounce. The previous two years we finished sixth. So we're close, very close.

We start against Gloucester tomorrow and the Championship will be our main target. It's still the blue riband event for first-class cricketers. But since 1968, we've won just three trophies, the NatWest (or Gillette Cup as it was in those days) in 1969, the JPS Sunday League in 1983 and the Benson and Hedges Cup in 1987 so we're hungry for silverware in any competition, whether it's the NatWest, the new National League or the Super Cup.

Our resident superstar Darren Gough will be around to get us off to a flier against Gloucester and again when we make our bow as Yorkshire Phoenix, complete with bright orange strip, in our first game in the National League on Sunday. Then he'll be away to link up with England and their World Cup preparations. Gavin Hamilton, who will be playing for Scotland, leaves us after the Championship game against Somerset which starts next Thursday. We'll miss them, of course, and there's every chance that they could both be involved in the Test series against New Zealand later in the summer. So might Michael Vaughan after his great winter tour as England A captain.

But I firmly believe we still have a line-up strong enough to win trophies. And that's the first time I've said so with real conviction since I joined the staff 15 years ago.

In all that time I have never known a Yorkshire squad with such strength in depth in all departments, or a group of players with such a great team spirit and positive attitude. It hasn't happened overnight; it's been building up for four or five years now. But after finishing third last season, we're ready to take the final step forward.

With Greg Blewett taking over from Darren Lehmann as our overseas player, and Richard Harden signed from Somerset to reinforce the middle order, there's really tough competition for batting places.

But it's in the seam bowling department that we will be the envy of every other county. Goughie and Chris Silverwood are England fast bowlers and Paul Hutchison, who should be fit after a back injury by the middle of May, has twice toured with England A. Hamilton was a revelation last season, Matthew Hoggard is the best prospect I've ever seen, and Ryan Sidebottom is a left-armer like Hutch who can introduce variety. To think I used to play in the same side as his dad!

Then, of course, there's Craig White, who's fit again after last season's back trouble and can be as quick as anyone, and Blewett, who's a more than useful seam bowler. Silvers, who's had a bit of a neck niggle, hasn't been chosen for the opening game and Ryan misses out, too. Their chance will come. But on an early-season pitch at Headingley I'm confident we'll have enough firepower to start with a win. Weather permitting, of course.

On the evidence of Yorkshire's first outing, Blakey's optimism is justified. After being put in to bat on an overcast Headingley morning, they overcame a shaky start, in which Blewett was dismissed cheaply, to reach 80. Hamilton, who shared an important seventh wicket stand of 66 with Blakey, top-scored with 81 not out before claiming 4 for 26 as Gloucester were dismissed for 169. After rain, Yorkshire's declaration set their opponents a target of 262 in 72 overs. Gough and Hamilton bowled Yorkshire to victory with ten overs to spare.

PPP County Championship, Headingley. 21–24 April. Yorkshire 280 (G.M. Hamilton 81 not out) and 148–6 dec. beat Gloucestershire 169 (Hamilton 4–26) and 180 (D. Gough 4–27, Hamilton 3–33) by 81 runs. Yorkshire 18 pts, Gloucester 4 pts.

CGU National League, Headingley. 25 April. Yorkshire Phoenix 147–8 (C. White 49) beat Gloucestershire Gladiators 145 (White 4–25) by 2 wickets.

An impressive start. We couldn't have asked for more. Two games, two wins. Our groundsman Andy Fogarty worked miracles to have the pitch ready for the Championship game but it was still a real grafter's wicket when 20 was worth 50 on another day. We reckoned 250 would be a good total so 280 was a bonus. And, as I predicted, we had too much power for Gloucester in our seam battery.

But the match was a disaster for our new signing, Dick Harden. He was hit on the left hand by a ball from Jon Lewis that lifted off a length. Welcome to Headingley! It's badly broken, he needs an operation and he's going to be out for six weeks. Dick is devastated.

He joined us from Somerset during the winter although it's fair to say that the signing wasn't universally popular in the dressing-room or among the membership. The Yorkshire Academy churns out a lot of talented young players and many people questioned the wisdom of bringing in a 33-year-old who had been released by his previous county after an indifferent season. They were worried about the kind of signal Harden's arrival sent to the young players.

I don't see it that way. One of our weaknesses last season was in the middle order, particularly in the one-day game. You don't have any time to come in and have a look and if we'd had an experienced player who could manipulate the ball around we might have won another four or five games. That is one of Harden's strengths. And as well as being an excellent one-day player, he's scored almost 13,000 first-class runs in 14 seasons at an average of nearly 40. A lot of those runs have been against Yorkshire. He's a good team man, a good thinker and he's introduced some new ideas into the dressing-room already.

He's signed a two-year contract after which he will be emigrating to New Zealand, where his wife comes from. But he has shown enough already to prove that he isn't here for the ride. He's hugely impressed with our set-up and desperate to do well for Yorkshire and help us win something.

And above all, his arrival has beefed up the competition for places in the middle of the order – and that can only be a good thing. Assuming Blewie and Vaughan, or Virgil as we call him because he speaks just like the character from Thunderbirds, will open, with the captain, David Byas, at number three, we will have Dick, Matthew Wood, Anthony McGrath, Bradley Parker and young Gary Fellows fighting for two places.

Understandably, perhaps, McGrath (Mags to everyone inside and outside the dressing-room) wasn't happy about the situation as it developed over the winter and asked to be released. Predictably, the answer was no. He is a fine player, good enough to tour with England A twice. But he would be the first to admit that he hasn't scored enough runs over the last couple of years.

When Martyn Moxon retired before the start of last season he had a marvellous chance to establish himself as Vaughan's opening partner but he never really got going and eventually lost his place in the side for the second year in a row. To his credit, he's knuckled down and worked ever so hard over the winter. He's been playing in Australia and he's seemed really sharp in training and on our pre-season tour of South Africa. Technically he's looking a million dollars again so he was bitterly disappointed to miss out in the first game against Gloucester.

But he's not the first person to discover that a week is a long time in sport and Dick's misfortune has opened a door for Mags. Now it's up to him to score a mountain of runs and make it impossible for the captain to leave him out again. Ironically, his first chance will come against Somerset in our second Championship game, starting on Thursday. Richard Harden's old club.

SOMERSET V YORKSHIRE, TAUNTON

Wednesday, 28 April. En route to Taunton and an afternoon net before the start of Yorkshire's second Championship game of the season tomorrow. On Sunday night, Bank Holiday weekend, Yorkshire will head north for a National League game against Worcester at New Road on Monday. This weekend's cricket marks the start of Yorkshire's Gough-free zone. He will be away with the England World Cup squad until, hopefully, the final on 20 June.

Goughie! He may be one of the gold-plated megastars of world cricket but here he's just one of the lads. For the last four seasons or so, we've had a Phantom Sock Snipper in the dressing-room who strikes by snipping the end off players' socks. Or alternatively, he cuts the crutch out of their underpants. All good schoolboy stuff, I know, but the Phantom has given us a load of laughs in his time. If Goughie wasn't away with England so often, he'd be one of the favourites in the Phantom Sock Snipper stakes although, to be fair, his style of prank lacks the Phantom's subtlety. His jokes tend to be a bit on the obvious side and you always know he's behind it because he can't keep a straight face.

From my vantage point behind the stumps I've seen just about every ball he's bowled for Yorkshire since he made his first-class début against Middlesex at Lord's on 20 April 1989, when he finished with match figures of 5 for 91, impressed a lot of people and *Wisden's* verdict was that he began his first-class career 'in some style'. On that occasion David Bairstow was keeping wicket but Goughie only played in a couple of first-class games that season because of injury and I've been wicketkeeper for virtually all his Yorkshire career since then. So I've had a better view than anyone in the world of the way he has developed from a raw youngster fresh out of the Yorkshire Academy into one of the game's leading fast bowlers.

I first saw him in action in the indoor school. He was a YTS trainee who joined the Academy when it started in 1989. He was always a strong lad and he used to just run in and let it go. Like most young fast bowlers there wasn't a lot of control; it was a question of getting it down to the other end as fast as he could. You could see he could swing the ball and had good variation but putting them together wasn't his strength. You can say that about a lot of young bowlers, of course, and at that time there was no gut feeling among the rest of the staff that Yorkshire had unearthed a real world beater.

It wasn't until we played down in Somerset in 1994 that I started to think, 'We've got something a bit special here.' The wicket was quite dry and conditions shouldn't have been helping him. But he suddenly produced this slower ball that we hadn't really seen before and he bowled Somerset out, taking 7 second innings wickets for 42 to finish the game with match figures of 10 for 96. At one stage in Somerset's second innings, he had figures of 3 for 0 from 13 deliveries.

And in the one-day games he was beginning to bowl people out with the in-swinging yorker that has now become his trademark. Any bowler can try and bowl a yorker but not many get it right consistently like Goughie. They bowl it too full or too short, get the line wrong and end up being hit away on the legside. Darren's yorker is like a missile. He starts it off on a good line, then it swings in viciously towards the leg stump. The swing is very late, which makes the delivery exceptionally difficult to play. To be able to produce it more or less when he wants is an incredible talent.

He's a bit like Ian Botham as a bowler, if not as a batter. He is always capable of producing a wicket out of nowhere and changing the course of a game. He's never going to be content bowling line and length and taking wickets by building up pressure on the batsmen. He'll just come on and if it's his day – and it usually is – he'll take wickets for you. He's good for a couple at the top of the order but because of the yorker he's devastating against the tail.

He likes me to tell him he's bowling fast. I usually have a quiet word at the end of an over. He'll switch off if I start to get technical and offer advice about how the batsman is playing or where to probe in the next few overs. It's pace that makes him tick. Raw pace! So instead I'll say, 'Bloody hell, Goughie, you were really hitting the gloves there!' and he'll give me a big grin and start talking about speedometers and topping 90 mph. Then he'll head off back to the third man boundary with a big smile, fired up for the next assault.

We have one or two top secret signals between us, particularly for his slower ball. For obvious reasons I'm not going to disclose it here and if I'm totally honest I have to admit that for one reason or another the channel of communication breaks down more often than not.

Goughie claims the signal is as clear as the nose on your face but as a rule, I'm chatting to the captain and Craig White in the slips or we've got better things to look at than Darren's backside disappearing into the middle distance. So when the slower ball arrives we have been known to be standing four or five yards too deep. You'd expect England's premier fast bowler to get a bit upset but he just shakes his head knowingly, gives us a rueful smile and trudges back to his mark.

I've always changed next to him since we moved from the old pavilion into our new dressing-rooms below the main stand at Headingley. Overseas player on one side, Goughie on the other. And you wouldn't believe the gear that's waiting for him every match. Boots, bats, tracksuits, mobile phones, everything. I try to slip some of it my way but he never misses a trick. He must have a warehouse somewhere to keep it all. And his mail! These days he employs his own secretary to answer all his letters.

I travelled with him for a couple of years when he first came into the side. He lived in a town house in Ossett and his pride and joy was a VW Convertible. That explains why we used to travel mainly in my car. But times have changed.

Now he drives a four-by-four and his wife has a BMW convertible and they live in something decidedly more palatial. He writes a column in the *News of the World* (mine is in the *Huddersfield Examiner*) and it sometimes seems as if the whole world is wanting to talk to him at the same time. But no one in our team would begrudge him his lifestyle. He's worked hard for it and as a top international sportsman he deserves everything he can get. It's a pity a few more cricketers don't

earn that kind of money – but that's a different story and I'll come back
to it later.

But as a person, Goughie hasn't really changed since the day he
made it into the Yorkshire side. We all arrived with parental advice but
apparently his dad's instructions were to 'keep it in your trousers, lad!'
Or words to that effect. We've often had a laugh about it since and on
the evidence of the nights out I enjoyed with him during his bachelor
days, I can reveal that he was never short of female admirers. He's
always been a good-looking lad.

It can't be easy for him coming back into the county game after
performing heroics for England but no one can question his
commitment. He'll work his bollocks off for Yorkshire. And if there's
any danger of him claiming superstar status in the dressing-room, the
lads bring him back down to earth with a bang.

Like the time he featured in a national newspaper column about
cooking. Each week, the paper featured a famous personality from
various walks of life describing how they prepared their favourite dish.
Sure enough, there was Goughie revealing his secret recipe for chicken
casserole. It sounded delicious. But I can say with reasonable
confidence that Darren would not be totally at home trying to boil an
egg or open a can of beans, never mind a gourmet dish. So he had to
take some dreadful stick about that particular addition to the Gough
scrapbook. And despite all the talk about healthy eating, Goughie has
never been averse to the occasional donar kebab or, like any of the lads
on the circuit, an intake of fast food.

A few pints of lager don't go amiss, either. When he first arrived in
the side, he was a lager man, pure and simple, but fame and fortune
have seen him climb up the drinking ladder and now he claims to be
a fully paid-up member of the wine connoisseurs' brigade. I suspect
most of the bottles in his cellar are recommended on the back of a
Sainsbury's car park ticket, though.

He's even into champagne now. But again he fell foul of the lads
when he appeared with Chris Evans on *TFI Friday*, tasting three
different types of bubbly. One of them was Goughie's alleged favourite
vintage – but needless to say, he failed to pick it out, much to the
hilarity of his team-mates.

And don't believe those stories about him being a frustrated soccer
superstar either. For some reason best known to himself, he's a Spurs

fan and listening to him talk about his footballing prowess, David Ginola's days in the White Hart Lane line-up are clearly numbered. Darren reckons he's a set-piece specialist who could easily have played professionally for Barnsley if cricket hadn't got in the way. But on the evidence of his performances in our training kick-abouts, I'm far from convinced. He's a bit short of pace and vision, for starters. We do have one or two half-decent footballers on the staff – in fact Anthony McGrath is an outstanding player – but Goughie looks pretty average to me. Skilful but lacking in workrate!

In fairness, though, he is a talented all-round sportsman . . . and he hits a golf ball a mile. He's a bit of a bandit, to put it mildly. But Goughie, being Goughie, he has to have all the fancy gear and he loves nothing better than playing with the big boys in the pro-celebrity events. He has to take endure his share of stick about that, too.

It's all good-natured stuff, though. Because Goughie is very popular with the rest of the boys and he's good fun to have around. He always has been. What you see is what you get. He plays the game with a smile on his face and gives off the right vibes. He's a big, bustling Barnsley lad who's done well and he doesn't really pretend to be anything else. No wonder he's so popular with the Yorkshire and England public; in fact with fans all over the world. He's captured people's imagination and they have taken him into their hearts. He's every kid's favourite cricketer and a great ambassador for his sport. And his favourite film? 'Bridge over Navarone'. Nice one, Darren!

PPP County Championship, Taunton. 30 April–2 May. Somerset 468–9 dec. (J. Cox 173) and 26–4. Yorkshire 148 and 345 (D. Byas 90, A. McGrath 75). Somerset won by 6 wickets.
CGU National League, Worcester. 3 May. Yorkshire Phoenix 213–7 (D. Byas 87) beat Worcestershire Royal 212–5 (D. Leatherdale 70, G. Haynes 66) by 3 wickets.

Very disappointing. With hindsight it was a mistake to put them in when we won the toss but there looked to be enough moisture in the wicket for our pace attack to exploit. Instead, Jamie Cox, their new overseas man from Tasmania, took us to the cleaners and their bowlers used the conditions better than we did. Simple as that. At one stage we looked as if we might get back into it in the second innings with Byas getting close to his first ton of the season and McGrath proving a point with a quality half century. But in the end we got what we deserved. The National League win at Worcester on Monday at least gave us something to smile about on the way home but we need to get the Somerset performance out of our system quickly.

YORKSHIRE V INDIA, HARROGATE. WORLD CUP WARM-UP

Sunday, 9 May. St George's Road, Harrogate. Yorkshire are due to play India in a warm-up game for the World Cup. As supporters arrive on a pleasant morning, keen to be re-united with Sachin Tendulkar, Yorkshire's first overseas player and now by common consent the world's best batsman, they are stunned to learn there will be no play. The match is abandoned without a ball bowled because water has seeped under the covers overnight. Tendulkar and his team-mates leave for a net at Headingley. Harrogate officials, keen to impress the cricket world in their bid to restore first-class cricket at the ground, are understandably devastated.

A fiasco. Eight months away from a new millennium and we can't keep a few acres of grass dry enough for a game of cricket. I feel sorry for the Harrogate club because this was going to be a huge day for them. No doubt people will argue about who was to blame for weeks to come. Was it Harrogate's responsibility? Or Yorkshire's? I don't know and I don't particularly care. All I know is that the Indians have missed an important practice match, the Yorkshire players have lost out on a chance to take on some of the world's best players and, above all, the fans are the ultimate losers.

But this weekend's events will only fuel the flames of the argument against taking Yorkshire cricket back to the outgrounds. At the annual meeting it was a desperately close vote with the members eventually calling on the committee to 'consider' returning to Harrogate and

Sheffield next year. To put it mildly, today hasn't helped the outgrounds' case.

Let me say straight away where I stand on the issue: I do not want to go back to the outgrounds. I feel very strongly about it and I'm sure 90 per cent of the Yorkshire squad feel exactly the same way. We want to play the majority of our cricket at Headingley with a couple of games at Scarborough. We believe that arrangement gives us the best chance of winning cricket matches – which is what Yorkshire County Cricket Club is supposed to be all about. I also believe that the players' views should be heard and taken into account.

Since I became a Yorkshire player in 1985 I have been fortunate, sorry, that should be unfortunate, enough to play on the outgrounds at Hull, Bradford, Middlesbrough, Sheffield and Harrogate. And quite simply, the facilities for the players are not up to standard. We are professional sportsmen and the least we are entitled to are professional-standard facilities to give us the best chance of performing to the best of our ability and win matches for Yorkshire.

When we played at Bradford we didn't even have a pavilion. We changed in an underground bunker that the local dogs used as a toilet overnight. Each morning the stench was revolting. There was no players' viewing area so the next batsman in had to sit on the open terrace; if the weather was cold he would just have to grin and bear it. Going out to face a Test fast bowler with a stiff back and frozen fingers is no fun, believe me. There was no car parking and we could never be 100 per cent sure whether our cars would be in one piece when we got back to them. In the end, Bradford gave up trying to fight a losing battle.

At Sheffield, we had 12 players with God knows how much gear trying to get changed in about nine square yards of space, falling over one another's equipment, cursing and swearing. The showers weren't up to the mark and there usually weren't enough towels to go round. The physio's couch had to be put outside on the balcony.

Once, when we were playing at Abbeydale Park, the scorers had to introduce a unique entry into the day's card – deer stopped play. It came bounding out of the woods at the top side of the ground. Then it hurtled past Anthony McGrath at cover, skidded across the square with no regard for the wicket, and crashed into the mobile covers at the bottom of the ground before heading back into the forest. An interesting diversion to put it mildly.

The dressing-room facilities at Harrogate are not much better. The showers are poor, the toilet stinks and again there's no room for the physio to work properly if we need treatment. If you take a stroll round the ground and sit down and chat with members or friends you're likely to end up with splinters in your backside.

I don't blame the clubs involved because I appreciate how hard their officials and members work and how many hours they put in. I realise there simply isn't the money around to change what are basically league grounds into first-class arenas. And yes, in years gone by, some of the greatest names in Yorkshire cricket history have won games and championships on the outgrounds and no one has complained. Not for the record, anyway.

But this is 1999. Standards have improved in all areas of life, including professional sport. And the least players are entitled to is comfortable accommodation, a place to park the car, your own peg in the dressing-room, a bit of space to get changed, a gym to work out in, a treatment room if you pick up a knock, a decent shower at the end of the day and the right kind of food and drink available. We were third in the Championship last season, the position occupied by Chelsea in this year's FA Premiership. But would you expect the Chelsea players to play 50 per cent of their games out in the sticks? Would they be expected to perform to the best of their ability if some of their so-called home games were played in sub-standard stadiums? OK, who knows where they might be asked to play in an FA Cup-tie away from home – and that's part of the charm of the competition. It's the same in our NatWest Trophy when we have to go and play a Minor County. But for home games we're surely entitled to the best possible facilities.

But I dare say we would put up with some of the shortcomings if we could be sure the outgrounds offered us the best chance of winning. Today's problems with the covers at Harrogate have underlined one of the dangers. It has happened before at St George's Road – in fact, last year the Costcutter Cup final was reduced to a bowl-out because one end of the square was sodden after heavy rain. Even though the sun was shining, the playing area was unfit and understandably the players didn't fancy it. They had the same weather down the road at Headingley yet we completed a Benson and Hedges semi-final.

And we've suffered the same scenario at Sheffield where rain has run down the slope, left damp patches on the square and we've spent six hours sitting around doing nothing. Imagine that happening on the final day of a crucial county game with Yorkshire needing a couple of wickets for maximum points and you'll appreciate the potential problems and frustrations.

On top of that, when we arrive at one of the outgrounds we might just as well be playing an away game. We have little or no idea how the pitch will play, certainly no more than the opposition. So the toss tends to be a lottery.

So what's so special about Headingley? As far as the spectators are concerned, not a lot. I accept that. And I was wholeheartedly behind the proposed move to Wakefield which now appears to have bitten the dust. That would have given players, members and cricket lovers a state-of-the-art twenty-first century stadium with the best possible facilities on and off the field. Of course there was opposition from the traditionalist lobby, just like there was when my hometown football club, Huddersfield Town, decided to leave their outdated old Leeds Road ground and move to the McAlpine Stadium. There was uproar. But the objectors only needed five minutes in the new stadium to realise what they had been missing. Cricket should be ready to follow that lead. And not just in Yorkshire.

For the time being, though, the players here believe that Headingley offers us the best chance of winning games. That's the bottom line. Off the field we are comfortable for all the reasons that make us uncomfortable at the outgrounds and if that might mean the difference between winning and losing we have to go for it.

But above all, we know every inch of Headingley where it matters – out there in the middle. Our coach Martyn Moxon and captain David Byas work closely with the groundsman Andy Fogarty in pitch preparation and he has produced wickets with plenty of pace and bounce that will suit our seam attack and, given a break with the weather, produce results. That's not a fiddle. Every county is entitled, within the regulations, to prepare wickets to suit its playing strengths and now we've even managed to put a bit of life into the pitches at Scarborough as well. The old shirt fronts that produced well over 1,000 runs and not a lot of wickets in a four-day game are a thing of the past. And rightly so, too. Those run feasts were a total bore for the players so I dread to think what the spectators thought. At Yorkshire, we believe in result pitches – and if the result goes against us, so be it. We'd rather lose a match by going for a win than play out a mind-numbing draw on a flat pitch.

And at Headingley we know all the angles. We know exactly when and where we can turn a two into a three, how the ball will run on different parts of the outfield, how close to stand for each individual bowler. On their own these may seem little things but believe me, they can add up to the small advantage that might make all the difference between winning and losing a game and even a championship or a one-day competition. They are factors that must not be ignored.

The committee have known the players' feelings for some time. But this year David Byas decided to speak out in favour of Headingley and Scarborough before the annual meeting. He was giving the players' view, nothing more nor less. And surely he had every right to do so. We are the people who have to go out there and try to win cricket matches. Yet from the outraged response in some quarters you would have thought he had called for the return of the death penalty and the abolition of the monarchy. It was the Peasants' Revolt all over again. Members wrote to the local media demanding how dare a man who is no more than a paid employee of the club express an opinion on an important cricketing issue? Even if he is the county captain.

What a ridiculous state of affairs! The players have a right to be heard and if the members choose to ignore their views, so be it. But we're still entitled to express them. And I might as well say here and now that anyone who believes players should be seen and not heard might as well stop reading. Because there's plenty more where that came from.

World Cup warm-up. Yorkshire v India, Harrogate. 9 May. Match abandoned.

YORKSHIRE V SCOTLAND, SCARBOROUGH. WORLD CUP WARM-UP

Wednesday, 12 May. The World Cup warm-up programme moves on to Scarborough where Yorkshire entertain a Scotland side boasting the all-round talents of Yorkshire's own Gavin Hamilton.

Ouch! Gavin's World Cup almost ended before it began thanks to a beamer from Craig White. Accidental, of course. It just slipped out but Chalkie can be decidedly quick and Gavin never picked it up. The helmet clanged and the Flower of Scotland was spread-eagled on the North Marine Road turf. It looked nasty for a moment because he just lay completely still. There was the proverbial deathly hush around the ground.

Players are inevitably concerned when a batsman goes down and it was even worse knowing he was one of our own team-mates. But after a couple of minutes, Gavin picked himself up, dusted himself down, called for a new helmet and got on with the job again. We all breathed a sigh of relief. In retrospect, the incident would turn out to be one of those rare moments of tranquillity in the waking life of G.M. Hamilton.

We haven't had many since he established himself in the side early last season and the dressing-room is going to be a quieter place without him during the World Cup. He's one of those people who just can't stop talking on or off the field. He must eat budgie seed for breakfast. He also happens to be a hell of a cricketer.

He came to Yorkshire after making a bit of a name for himself as a teenager with Scotland. He was born in Broxburn near Edinburgh but his family moved south to Kent when he was a kid and he learned his cricket down there before Scotland picked him up. He joined the Yorkshire Academy on the recommendation of the Scotland coach Jim Love, a former Yorkshire player of course, in 1993, the season after we opened our doors to outsiders. Sachin Tendulkar, Richie Richardson and Hamilton were the first three foreigners along with our Manchester-born Yorkshireman Michael Vaughan and Richard Stemp from Worcestershire. And over the next few years Gavin gradually started to establish himself in the senior squad.

He could always play. But you could never be quite sure what the end product would be from day to day. Like Goughie, I've seen just about every ball he's bowled for us. At first he used to run in like a headless chicken with about 200 per cent enthusiasm and not a lot of thought about what he was really trying to do. If he got it right he could be devastating.

But it was either four for twenty or nought for plenty and there was no reliable way of knowing which one it would be. If the radar was wrong and the ball started travelling to all parts, Gavin used to get an even bigger head of steam up and keeping wicket was like being a goalkeeper, diving all over the place. His batting was the same. From the first ball he faced, he was always ready to try something different – and needless to say, it didn't always work out. When it did, though, the results were spectacular.

At the end of the 1997 season there was quite a bit of speculation that he might not be retained but Yorkshire kept faith with him and it has paid off in a big way. He earned a regular place when White picked up a back injury that restricted his bowling and he's never looked back.

The transformation over the last 12 months has been staggering and quite honestly, in all my years in the game I've never seen anything like it. He accepted the challenge of a regular place in the side and all of a sudden the penny dropped. He just clicked with bat and ball. He became a more composed and confident player almost overnight.

The same thing had happened with Goughie. Both players developed an aura of confidence and started to believe they would do well rather than just hope. As the wicketkeeper I could see it straight away in Gavin's bowling. He has a good out-swinger which will always get decent players out. And batting at seven and eight we're at the crease together a lot, too, so I could see the change in his batting.

There were quite a few times when we were five or six down for not much more than a hundred and me, Gavin and the tail would hang around long enough to post a useful total. He's a real handful to bowl at because he's prepared to take the bowlers on and he'll always try something unorthodox. We usually have a few laughs when we're out there together. In 15 years, I've never bagged the dreaded pair and when either of us gets off the mark we'll cross in mid-wicket and say, 'can't bag 'em now!'

His golden streak started off in the game against Glamorgan down at Cardiff last August when he made the two top scores in the match and took five wickets in each innings for figures of 10 for 112. He was on his way. And it just kept on getting better. He produced career-best bowling performances in each of his next two games finally setting a landmark with 7 for 50 and 4 for 22 as we hammered Surrey by 164 runs at Scarborough. He finished his first full season with 572 runs at 33.64, 56 wickets at 20.41 and a ring of confidence that marked him down as an international player of the future. In fact, there was talk of him squeezing into the England World Cup squad, never mind Scotland. He was certainly unlucky not to get an A tour last winter.

I'll be very surprised if he doesn't do well in the World Cup. He runs on confidence and right now he's flying. This is his opportunity to test himself against some of the best players in the world and there's no reason why he shouldn't do well because he'll thrive on the extra responsibility of being Scotland's main man.

Despite the verbal diarrhoea and hyperactivity, I like the guy a lot. Even if he does keep running me out. He's great to have around and good for the team on and off the field. One of the lads once christened him the Club Dickhead. It was just a bit of fun and no one enjoyed the joke more than Gav. He's got an opinion on everything and will pass it on to anyone who's prepared to listen. Or, for that matter, someone who isn't. If you're having a quiet chat in the dressing-room, he'll come in and join in immediately. And usually he's got the wrong end of the stick. He's always taking the mickey out of the other players, cracking silly jokes or coming out with the bullshit. Talking, talking, talking.

As far as I know he's the only first-class cricketer who supports

Falkirk and rumour has it (not denied by Hamilton himself, of course) that he was once on Arsenal's books as a YTS trainee. No chance! That's the budgie seed working overtime again. He isn't good enough to be in Yorkshire's first-choice football team, never mind Arsenal.

But cricket is a very different story and we'll be hearing a lot more of Gavin in years to come. If he has a good World Cup he'll no doubt be in strong contention for a place in the England side for the series against New Zealand later in the summer. He's the type of aggressive genuine all-rounder we haven't really produced since Ian Botham, although I'd resist the temptation to throw him in just yet. Let him complete another season at Championship level and if he continues to improve at the same rate take him to South Africa next winter. Then watch the sparks fly.

World Cup warm-up, Scarborough. 12 May. Yorkshire 131–5 (G.S. Blewett 57*) beat Scotland 126–9 (G.M. Hamilton 44) by 5 wickets.

YORKSHIRE V MIDDLESEX, HEADINGLEY

Friday, 14 May. It has been a stop-start opening to the season which has left Yorkshire desperately in need of match practice before the important Championship game against Middlesex which starts at Headingley today. A frustrating time for players and supporters.

The early-season fixture list has been a total mish-mash, to put it politely. There's no logical reason why the first-class cricket season can't open with a full nine-match programme. Instead, on Wednesday, 13 April, we got under way with five Championship games. Another started the following day and a couple of matches against the universities were thrown in as well. That meant four counties, including Yorkshire, were not involved in the first programme of the season. The following week, eight Championship matches started on three different days. For the last ten days or so, we've all been involved in World Cup warm-up games. It's confusing for the players and even more confusing for the fans. And looking down the fixture list, it's going to carry on like this until September.

And if that isn't bad enough, the new National League, complete with coloured clothing, team nicknames and all the rest of the razzmatazz, crept furtively on to the scene with just one match, Leicester against Hampshire, on Saturday, 17 April with the attention of 90 per cent of the sporting public concentrating on the climax to the football season. There were three more fixtures the following day but once again a major cricket competition started without a full programme.

The National League is supposed to be the brave new world of cricket, the game that will attract a new, younger audience to our sport. And later on, I'll explain why I'm 100 per cent in favour of the idea. But surely it deserved a high-profile start with fireworks, celebrity stars and all the rest of the entertainment package. Instead, what did we have? One game. I'm sure my colleagues at Media Works, a Leeds-based marketing and PR company where I work during the winter, could have come up with something a bit more spectacular to launch cricket twenty-first century-style.

So far, four weeks after the official start of the season we've managed two Championship games, two in the National League, a rained-off match with India and the Scotland game at Scarborough. There's been no chance to find a rhythm and there's a danger that some of the hard work we put in over the winter will go down the pan.

And when I say hard work, I mean hard work. There's still a belief in some quarters that county cricketers just roll up at the beginning of April, have a few nets and a few pints and then away we go on to the summer treadmill. That's a million miles away from reality. In fact, the preparations for this season began within a few days of last season ending.

This is the schedule: at the end of September we go through a series of tests to assess our fitness levels, agility, speed, endurance and so on. Six weeks later, the winter training schedule drops through the letter box. Thud! It sets out in detail what is expected of us between the middle of November and our return at the beginning of March and gives each individual his own programme of running and gym work.

Like everyone else, I dread the running. For the fast bowlers it means pounding out the long-distance stuff, four or five miles at a time. For me, it's more building up the fitness through quick sprints and shuttles; the kind of running I'll need as a wicketkeeper and batsman during the season. It can be a bit of a ball-ache but in the final analysis no one has come up with a better form of aerobic fitness training so it has to be done.

There are regular checks to make sure no one is cutting any corners. Having said that, there are ways and means. Peter Hartley, who joined Hampshire at the end of the 1997 season, was a master at throttling back a bit during the first check-up of the winter and then he could ease himself up through the gears as the start of the new season approached. I don't know whether he pulled the wool over anyone's eyes or not but over a long, hard season he always managed to bowl as many overs as the next man – even if there were times when he could hardly get out of bed in the morning. I know. I used to room with 'Jack' and it wasn't a pretty sight.

This year, my own serious countdown started at six o'clock in the morning on Monday, 4 January. Happy New Year! I was on the road by 6.30 a.m., into the gym in Leeds at 7.15, and after a 90 minute work-out, time for a shower before reporting for duty at Media Works at nine o'clock. Same again, five days a week until the start of pre-season training on 1 March. The glamour of professional sport! Ginola, Giggs and Beckham eat your hearts out. I suppose people will find it hard to believe that a first-class cricketer's training programme involves such unsociable hours but for me, it has become a way of life.

As a Yorkshire player I'm only paid between March and October so all my winter fitness work goes down as a labour of love. But I've no complaints. This kind of intensive preparation has helped me put together a run of 104 consecutive County Championship games between August 1992, and the end of last season.

I'm not pretending I've been a perfect physical specimen in every one of those appearances; in fact you could probably count on one hand the number of games when I haven't been carrying a minor niggle of one sort or another. But maintaining a high level of fitness has been a vital factor. And while getting up at six o'clock on a winter morning can be a pain in the arse, it's a small sacrifice to make.

Needless to say, our pre-season regime is a million miles away from my first season on the staff in 1984. The cream of Yorkshire cricket turned up on 1 April with the senior players going into one dressing-room, the youngsters into another. Two laps of the field, a few sprints in front of the football stand and then break for a cup of tea. Out again for some high catching and fielding work and then inside for lunch and a chat. Follow that with an afternoon net and away in time to beat the rush-hour. For better or worse, things have progressed a bit since then.

PPP Healthcare County Championship, Headingley. 14–17 May. Yorkshire 160 (D. Byas 62) and 313 (A. McGrath 142, G.S. Blewett 73) lost to Middlesex 249 (M. Ramprakash 84, M. Hoggard 4–56) and 226–5 (J.S. Langer 127*) by 5 wickets.

Quite simply we didn't score enough runs in the first innings and were always chasing the game from there. But a good game of cricket on a result pitch and right until the last half hour or so I thought we might sneak it. We batted poorly in the first innings but Mags got us back into it with a smashing century on the third day. As I said before the Somerset game, Dick Harden's injury has given Mags his big chance and he's taken it.

His knock left Middlesex needing 224 and when we had five down with only 80-odd on the board it looked as if we would win it. But their Australian Justin Langer wasn't going to give it away and saw them home with a high-quality hundred; as good a fourth day innings as you'll see. Afterwards he singled out Chris Silverwood as the fastest bowler he has faced – and he's been in against Pakistan and the West Indies over the winter. As Yorkshire's wicketkeeper, I'll second the motion. Silvers, or Spoons as we sometimes call him, got everything right in this game and at times his pace was awesome. On this form there isn't a better fast bowler around. Definitely an England player this season.

ESSEX V YORKSHIRE, CHELMSFORD

Tuesday, 19 May. Little more than 24 hours after the end of the Middlesex game, Yorkshire are on the road again. This time to Chelmsford where, over the next five days, they will meet Essex in the Championship and National League.

The Middlesex game ended at around three o'clock yesterday afternoon, Monday. Now it's 6 p.m. on Tuesday and I'm in the passenger seat of Chris Silverwood's car on the way to Chelmsford. In the intervening 27 hours I've washed and ironed my kit, packed three suitcases, sorted out one or two bits of admin that have inevitably built up during the Middlesex game, written my weekly column for the *Huddersfield Examiner*, had a session with Andrew Collomosse, who's co-writing this book with me, and had a couple of hours in the nets working on the batting. Oh and yes – I managed a bite to eat, a few hours' sleep and some time with my partner Clare.

Pick a day, any day, during the summer months and it's a safe bet there will be county cricketers like me and Spoons hurtling up and down the motorways in pursuit of their trade. I'd love to add up how many miles we put in between us over a season. In the end, though, we accept it as just part of the job. I suppose if your mythical sports enthusiast from Mars arrived on Earth and discovered that some of the best cricketers in the world are forced to include five hours of motorway madness in their match preparation, he'd think we'd all gone quietly barmy.

The footballing élite are cosseted in luxury coaches with all mod cons while Test cricketers check out the road map, switch on the ignition and hit the road. It's no fun driving home from Canterbury or Taunton after a full day in the field – even if you've won. It was even worse, though, when we played 24 three-day matches in a season. There were some real nightmare trips, believe me.

I remember once finishing a game at Eastbourne at about 6 p.m. then jumping in the car and driving up to Middlesbrough. We arrived at about three o'clock in the morning, snatched a few hours' sleep, reported at the ground for practice at 9 a.m., lost the toss and found ourselves facing a full day in the field. We once started a Championship game in Hastings on a Saturday, drove across to Bristol for a Sunday League game and then back to the south coast to resume the Championship match on the Monday. There was another time when we played 27 days' consecutive cricket at the height of summer. Crazy!

Coach travel would be one way to ease the stress factor but it's not as simple as that. Unlike football, we aren't just involved in a one-off 90 minute match. We can be away for anything up to a week playing two or three different games and using different players. If injuries crop up, we'll need to send the damaged player home and whistle up a replacement. The car is the easiest way for everyone.

On top of that, the Yorkshire players live all around the county and it's often far more convenient to set off from home rather than report to a central point before leaving together. Michael Vaughan lives in Sheffield, for instance, and there wouldn't be much point in him driving to Leeds to catch a bus back south again. It's the same with the captain and Chalkie, who live in east Yorkshire and have their own weird and wonderful routes to all points north, south and west. Over the years I've lived in three or four different parts of the county so it's a question of finding out who's my nearest team-mate before the season starts and linking up from there. This time, Spoons has drawn the short straw. A bus would be OK for a one-off one-dayer on the south coast but by and large life's a lot easier if we make our own arrangements.

I mentioned the washing and ironing, secretly hoping readers might not notice. It doesn't exactly fit the macho image of the professional sportsman, after all. But needs must and you'll find quite a lot of cricketers around who are a dab hand with the iron. Wives and partners help, of course, but they're not always in the right place at the right time and the prospect of washing five sets of sweaty kit week in and week out does have a limited appeal.

So when I got home last night, the kit went into the tub and this morning out came the iron. And then the packing operation began. We're playing a four-day game and a one-dayer against Essex so this is what I've got stashed away in the back of the car. For the Championship game: four shirts, four pairs of trousers, six pairs of socks, four sets of underwear, one long-sleeved sweater, one sleeveless sweater, tracksuit, three pairs of boots for various conditions underfoot, one pair of trainers, four pairs of wicketkeeping gloves, four pairs of batting gloves, batting pads, wicketkeeping pads, thigh pad, inner thigh pad, chest guard, four jock straps, one box (and what great value that's been for the two quid I paid six years ago), cap, sunhat, helmet, four bats, sunglasses, sunblock. For the National League game: (all in Yorkshire Phoenix colours), shirt, trousers, socks, batting pads, wicketkeeping pads, cap, sunhat, long-sleeved sweater, sleeveless sweater, tracksuit, trainers. Then there's a suit on a hanger because we have to report at the ground each morning looking immaculate, or that's the idea anyway, and a separate case with all the off-duty clothes, underwear etc. I don't take the iron.

PPP Healthcare County Championship, Chelmsford. 19–22 May. Yorkshire 311 (M.P. Vaughan 100) and 435–5 dec. (M.P. Vaughan 151) beat Essex 335 (S.G. Law 159) and 237 (S.G. Law 113, I.D. Fisher 5–73) by 74 runs.
CGU National League, Chelmsford. 23 May. Yorkshire Phoenix 223–7 (M.J. Wood 48) beat Essex Eagles 220 by 3 wickets.

The Championship match was a personal triumph for Michael Vaughan, who put an uncertain start to the season behind him in the most emphatic style by scoring a century in each innings. Remarkably, so did Essex's Australian all-rounder Stuart Law, only the second time in Yorkshire's history that a player from both sides has scored a century in each innings.

It goes without saying that Virgil batted well. So did Law, for that matter. Before the game Michael was starting to get a bit desperate. He had a great tour as captain of England A in Zimbabwe and South Africa and was on everyone's shortlist for a Test place this summer, but until this game hadn't been able to get a start at all.

In his situation, players try to put on a brave face but the doubts begin to creep in. You work at all sorts of little adjustments in the nets but the longer it goes on, the harder it becomes. In the end, you literally start to wonder where the next score is going to come from and you find yourself scratching around in the middle and getting nowhere. Michael hadn't reached that stage but I knew he was starting to feel a bit twitchy about it when he went down to Chelmsford. Then click, all of a sudden the world's a happier place.

I'm not taking anything away from his performance but the way he and Law stroked the ball around just reinforces what I've always said about pitches at this stage of the season. Down in the south, they're hard, true, bouncy and if you get it through the infield it's four. A different world and the batsmen can play with confidence virtually from day one. In Yorkshire it's a whole new story with the ball seaming about all over the place.

In the home game against Middlesex both sides were scraping around trying to make 250 and there we were at Chelmsford knocking up 400 for 5 in our second dig. I've always said a 50 at Headingley in May is worth a 100 at somewhere like The Oval and nothing that's happened so far this season has made me change my mind.

The trouble is that people look at the scorecards, see the southern-based players are among the runs and immediately throw their names into the hat for England. Don't get me wrong, I'm not saying that people like Thorpe, Hussain and Stewart can't play because I know from watching them from behind the stumps all these years that they can. But so can Dave Byas and Michael Vaughan, to name just a couple. If Dave had played for Surrey instead of Yorkshire he'd have made a stack of runs and almost certainly become England's regular number three. Instead he's branded as nothing more than a good county player, and that's absolute nonsense.

Overall verdict on the Essex game – good to get back to winning ways although we're still a bit below par in both batting and bowling. Another excellent Sunday performance to make it three wins out of three from three close games. We were looking to chase 220 and by halfway that was up to seven an over. In years gone by we have just faded away in those situations but not any more. We all believed we would win it and we did.

YORKSHIRE V DURHAM, HEADINGLEY

Thursday, 27 May. After their successful sortie to the Home Counties, Yorkshire return to Headingley to take on Durham, against whom they have enjoyed conspicuous success since Durham's entry into the first-class arena in 1992. Last year was no exception, Yorkshire winning by nine wickets at The Riverside. In that game, Blakey claimed four victims behind the stumps en route to being the country's top wicketkeeper with 71 victims, 69 caught and two stumped.

A lot of people have congratulated me on topping the wicketkeeping charts. In terms of victims 1998 was the best year in my career and a good way to end my benefit season. But if the bowlers don't find the edge, I don't get any catches. So my success was down to Messrs Gough, Silverwood, Hamilton, White, Hutchison, Hoggard and Sidebottom, otherwise known as the best seam battery in the game.

People inevitably look at a wicketkeeper's total of victims and assess his season on that basis, but it doesn't work out like that. It's not the number of chances you take that counts – it's the number you miss. And people often say that the best wicketkeepers are the ones who go about their job quietly and unobtrusively.

I remember a few years back playing against Northants at Luton and they batted throughout the final day, making over 350 runs. In all that time, I didn't concede a bye and I didn't miss a single ball, either from the bowlers or fielders. Other members of the wicketkeepers' union will know I'm not boasting when I say it was a perfect display. As good as it gets. The best day of my career.

Yet no one . . . team-mates, opponents, scorers, Press, supporters or, for that matter, the tea ladies said a word. Not a single 'Well played, Blakes, you've had a good 'un today.' It's a different story when I shell a couple of chances, of course. And there are times when I keep wicket like a complete pillock, take one absolutely blinding catch and find people are all over me afterwards, saying what a marvellous day I've had. It's just part of the job, I suppose, and down the years the lads have started to appreciate what's involved a bit more.

Overall, though, I was happy with my performance last summer. But you can never afford to be complacent and before we reported back this time I asked Martyn Moxon to arrange a coaching session with Alan Knott. He's the best keeper this country has produced in the last 50 years and arguably the best of all-time. So if I say he's an even better coach, you'll have some idea about how highly I rate him. He encourages and coaxes and after a couple of hours with Knotty, you leave the nets believing you're the best wicketkeeper in the world. I worked with him on my two England A tours and the full tour to India in 1992–93 but I haven't seen him for a couple of years and want to brush up on one or two things.

That admission will no doubt please the Yorkshire member who used the occasion of the annual meeting at Huddersfield Town Hall in March to stand up and have a real go at me. The gist of his message was that Blakey never looks bothered either as a batsman or wicketkeeper and what were Yorkshire going to do about finding a replacement? He's entitled to his opinion but unfortunately I wasn't around to argue the case for the defence.

As it was David and Martyn both came out strongly in my favour with the captain pointing out that I had played in every game despite a string of niggling injuries that might easily have forced me out. He can say that again. There were times when I could hardly walk when I arrived at the ground for the warm-up. But I was prepared to take painkillers, something I'm not happy about in the long-term, and go out and give it 100 per cent. But outside the dressing-room, nobody knows about things like that. And I've never been one to make a fuss.

But while professional sportsmen always shrug aside criticism as water off a duck's back, it can hurt, particularly when it is ill-informed. No one in the Yorkshire team has ever criticised my attitude and I trust they never will. But outsiders sometimes look at me and claim I'm a bit too laid back. From the boundary edge, maybe, but who are they to say what's going on inside my head?

I suspect that part of the problem is that I took over as wicketkeeper from David Bairstow, one of the most bubbly characters Yorkshire cricket has ever produced. It's still hard to come to terms with his tragic death last January.

Bluey, as we always called him, was wicketkeeper and captain when I first broke into the side in 1985 but he was injured during my début against Middlesex at Headingley in the opening game of the season and I was asked to take over behind the stumps. Putting on his massive great stinking gloves was an eye-opening experience for an impressionable young player, believe me.

I had done a bit of wicketkeeping with Elland, my Huddersfield League club, but Steve Rhodes, who later moved on to Worcester and England, was the regular Second XI keeper so my chances were limited. But in that Middlesex game, I acquitted myself well enough for *Wisden* to comment: 'Richard Blakey, 18 and making his début, kept wicket in Bairstow's absence and held four catches, two of which were far from straightforward.'

David continued to suffer injury niggles over the next five seasons so I stood in on a regular basis, even though I had established myself at number three in the batting order and done well enough to be mentioned as an England player of the future. So it was a difficult decision when I was asked to do the job full-time in 1991.

On the one hand, was I compromising my chances of playing for England as a batsman? I'd already had two tours with England A and keeping wicket would inevitably mean moving down the order and reducing my chances of making really big scores. And what if I didn't measure up as a wicketkeeper after all?

On the other hand, I was a contracted Yorkshire player and I was being asked to do a job which the club felt would strengthen the side. So in the end I decided that if Richard Blakey keeping wicket was in the best interests of Yorkshire cricket I was happy to oblige. Looking back, I suppose I should have taken more time about the decision and consulted one or two people before finally making up my mind. But when you're young you tend to just go with the flow.

I talked to my mum and dad, of course. They have always been tremendously supportive right from the time when it was obvious my passion for sport would override my academic ambitions. I was a pretty good all-round sportsman as a kid and a round of golf on a Wednesday afternoon always had more appeal than my studies at Rastrick Grammar School. The headmaster disagreed – particularly after spotting that I had missed something like nine successive Wednesdays to join Paul Booth and Stuart Fletcher on the golf course. I might have got away with missing one afternoon . . . but nine?

I was a useful footballer, too, but after playing cricket for Yorkshire at all the junior age-group levels, playing professionally became my major ambition. So when the invitation to join the staff came along in 1982, I didn't need to be asked twice. And it was the same nine years later when I was given the chance to become first-choice wicketkeeper.

Inevitably, though, the one question I am asked more than any other is whether I have any regrets. The simple, honest answer is no. OK, sometimes, I wonder what might have been. Would I have gone on to score a mountain of runs and become a regular England player? Who knows? I could just as easily have disappeared from view like so many promising young cricketers. As it is, I've played five times for England, two Tests and three one-dayers, and that's something no one can ever take away from me. And there's absolutely no guarantee I would have achieved that purely as a batsman.

My early days as a keeper were a hard time, though. And one of the problems was my predecessor. For while David used to run around like a maniac, barking instructions that could be heard all over Leeds, never mind Headingley cricket ground, I adopted a less frantic approach – with the inevitable accusations from some quarters that I wasn't really bothered.

Yet if anything, I was far too wound up, both when I was standing in for Bluey and when I took over full-time. I was painfully aware that I was replacing a Yorkshire legend, a fantastic cricketer, a super keeper and a huge favourite with the crowd. I knew that comparisons were always being made and it was going to be hard for me to measure up to his standards.

I tried to concentrate for every minute of every innings and I allowed each small error to prey on my mind. I used to be totally drained at the end of a day's play. It took me a long time but eventually, I came to terms with the demands of the job and now I've got the concentration down to a fine art.

I start to concentrate when the bowler is halfway down his approach and then really switch on when he reaches the delivery stride. The maximum concentration span is no more than two-and-a-half seconds. Between deliveries I'll talk tactics and the state of the game with the close fielders or discuss the last ball and try to stay focused but relaxed until it's time for those crucial seconds of concentration on the next delivery.

I may look laid back and I'm sorry if some people get the wrong impression. Perhaps this season I should start charging down the wicket between overs, waving my arms around and bawling encouragement to the rest of the boys. It might make my critics feel better about me but I'd probably end up spilling a load of chances. So on balance, I'll stay as I am, thank you. And I can assure you that when we're out in the middle, no one is more tuned in to the game than I am.

PPP Healthcare County Championship, Headingley. 27–30 May. Yorkshire 310 (D. Byas 68, A. McGrath 62) and 16–1 beat Durham 114 (C. Silverwood 3–30, M. Hoggard 3–41) and 211 (C. White 4–63, C. Silverwood 3–45) by 9 wickets.
CGU National Cricket League, Headingley. 31 May. Yorkshire Phoenix 136–2 (C. White 67) beat Hampshire Hawks 132 (C. Silverwood 3–23) by 8 wickets.

Durham's batting simply wasn't up to the questions asked by our seam attack and we won it before lunch on the third day. And we annihilated Hampshire in the National League with one of the best bowling performances I've seen from Yorkshire in a one-dayer. We frustrated all their batsmen by giving them no width to hit through the ball and the wickets tumbled. And with only 130 to chase, Byas and White stroked the ball to all parts and we had the points sewn up in only 19 overs. This was Yorkshire at our best and if we carry on like this we're going to take a helluva lot of stopping.

DERBYSHIRE V YORKSHIRE, DERBY

Wednesday, 2 June. For the 1999 season, Blakey has adopted a new batting technique. In terms of figures, the results have not as yet been startlingly successful although observers have commented on what appears to be a more positive approach at the crease. The Championship game at Derby, in which the first day was lost to rain, saw him register his first half century of the season, an undefeated 70, as Yorkshire batted through the last day to earn a draw.

For the last couple of years I've been conscious that I haven't made as many Championship runs as I should. Last season it was 448 at an average of just over 21 with a highest score of 67 not out. The year before I did better with 670 at 37.22 with a top score of 90. But for someone who was once regarded as a potential Test batsman, the figures aren't good enough.

Batting at number seven doesn't help because opportunities are limited and I don't always get a chance to build an innings as I would like. And then again, the size of a batsman's score doesn't always reflect its importance in winning or saving a match. There are as many meaningless hundreds around as there are vital thirties. But from a personal point of view, I haven't reached three figures since 1996 and that's too long.

I thought about it long and hard over the winter. The basic problem is that I have been getting out caught behind the wicket or in the slips far too often. I wasn't getting my head in line with the ball and consequently playing away from my body. I knew I needed to get further across. I talked to Martyn Moxon about it and worked with the video machine. Without getting too far into the technicalities, it's basically been a question of shifting my stance further over to the off side to help me get my head in line with the ball.

Has it worked? I'll tell you in September. But generally speaking, yes. So far, so good. I'm getting into line better and playing straighter, although the number of runs hasn't improved vastly. In spells, I think I've played well without really getting a score and, as I mentioned earlier, batting down the order doesn't help. I've contributed two or three times towards winning the match, particularly in one-day cricket. And that's what really matters. But I'm confident things will come good.

It hasn't been like a golfer remodelling his whole swing, more a case of making minor adjustments. And it has to be said that all players adapt their technique as the years go by. Blakey 1999-style is a million miles away from the youngster who made his début back in 1985.

We come into the game young and confident and just play it naturally in the first couple of seasons or so. In many ways that's the best bet and if you look at the great players, most of them have succeeded in sticking to their basic technique. But it's a funny old game this. Nothing warps the mind like cricket and the older you get, the more you start to think about where you might be going wrong, analysing how you are getting out instead of putting it out of your mind and getting on with the next innings.

It isn't long before the doubts appear and you start to put yourself under unnecessary pressure. Playing for Yorkshire for 15 years hasn't helped, either, because the expectations are so high. But even if I can't get the ball off the square after three months of the season, I'll stick with the revised technique. You have to give things time.

PPP Healthcare County Championship, Derby. 2–5 June. Yorkshire 117 (P. De Freitas 4–37) and 308–8 dec. (A. McGrath 76, R.J. Blakey 70*) drew with Derbyshire 206 (M. Hoggard 5–47, C. Silverwood 4–59).

My second innings run-in with Dominic Cork created a bit of a stir among the Derbyshire members and with the Press. Corkie thought he'd got me caught by the keeper down the legside early on – but the umpire didn't agree. End of story as far as I was concerned. But Corkie wasn't a happy man and the verbals were flying around for the rest of the innings.

It doesn't worry me and I can give as good as I get. Players like Cork are never reluctant to start having a go because it helps them get fired up. Fair enough, if that's their style and as long as the abuse doesn't get personal. And to be fair to Cork, he bowled well. But they forget that it often helps to wind a batsman up if he's on the receiving end. To be honest, sledging has never bothered me and I learned a long time ago how important it is not to show you're rattled. Cork and the rest of the Derby players got the message in the end.

But it was an important innings for me. At the start of play on the final day we knew were going to have to bat it out to earn a draw and someone would have to play a long innings. Mags made runs again and then it was my turn. After the not out incident, Corkie was firing it in short and was bowling pretty quick. On his day he can be as sharp as anyone and this was probably the fastest bowling I've faced this season. I've a few bruises to tell the story but the bottom line is I survived to fight another day and we got away with the draw.

And once the hostilities were over, Cork and I shook hands, said well played and promptly forgot all about the aggro. That's the way it should be and the way I have always played the game. Cork and his team-mates spent three hours on a Saturday afternoon in early June trying to knock seven shades of shit out of me. My job was to stand up and be counted and make sure my side didn't lose the game.

In those situations, things are bound to get a bit heated; that's the nature of professional sport. But it was all over as soon as we were across the boundary rope and back in the dressing-room. That's a lesson some of the kids coming into the game would be well advised to learn.

It has to be said, though, that the level of sledging and banter has increased since I first started. There's always been a lot of chat out in the middle in any class of cricket and the Huddersfield League was no exception. But these days, the ability to abuse an opponent is regarded as part and parcel of a player's armoury.

There are two types of sledging. First, the basic insult – usually employed by fast bowlers at the end of their follow-through. Some pacemen give the impression of not being the brightest of individuals. So the best some of them can come up with is the long, hard stare followed by 'You useless effing so-and-so' or just a one-word reference to the male or female anatomy. It's a bit pathetic really and that kind of thing goes straight over my head.

Then there's the witty wind-up, usually fired across the batsman from behind the wicket to the cover area. These are considerably more interesting than the first type and sometimes it's hard to resist the temptation to join in. But the best policy is always to ignore any kind of remark aimed in your direction.

But as I say, sledging has increased to the point where I believe the players' attitudes to their fellow professionals leave a lot to be desired. In fact, it's downright bad. It's all part of English cricket trying to follow the Australian lead and I have to admit that I'm as guilty as the next man. But that doesn't mean I'm happy about the way things have gone.

As far as Yorkshire cricket is concerned, it's been seen as part of the toughening-up process. There was a time when we were regarded as a bit of a soft touch and a bit too nice to be winners. I know that sounds hard to believe when you're talking about the traditional hard-bitten Yorkshire cricket pro, but until a few years ago there was definitely a feeling among other sides that we were a good bunch of lads – but not a winning unit. For better or worse, that's all changed. Now we will give as good as we get and it's been drilled into us over the last few years to be as aggressive as the opposition – and a bit more on top.

That's one of the reasons why I never walk these days. There was a time when a batsman automatically set off back to the pavilion if it was obvious he had touched the ball on its way through to the keeper. And I was definitely a member of the walking fraternity. Ten or twelve years ago, there was a feeling that the umpires had a difficult enough job to do without batsmen staying at the crease when everyone in the ground had seen him play at a ball outside the off stump and heard the snick.

And, of course, there was a touch of gamesmanship involved. If a batsman was well known as a walker, the umpire would be less inclined to give him out if he hung around at the crease when the decision was a bit iffy.

Nowadays, though, no one walks, ever. I've seen batsmen caught at second slip who have stood their ground and waited for the finger to be raised. Now that really is going a bit far. But with caught-behind appeals, we let the umpire make the decision. And if he gets it wrong, so be it.

As a wicketkeeper, I know better than anyone whether a batsman has got a nick or not but if the decision goes against me, I just get on with the job. I'm not one of those players who turn round and accuse the batsman of cheating – but many fielders do, and then refuse to walk themselves when they get an edge. That's pure hypocrisy. But you would be amazed at the number of people around who seem to believe there's one rule for the batters and another for the fielders.

I suppose the poor attitude out in the middle is one of the reasons why the game has lost some of its comradeship. When I was a young player, there was a huge camaraderie among professional cricketers. As a matter of course you would have a drink and a chat with the opposition at the end of a day's play and perhaps even a meal together later on.

Nowadays, unless we're up against one of the northern sides or those dreaded Welshmen, we rarely mingle with players from the other team. I can count on one hand the number of times we socialised with the opposition last season and there's no reason to suppose things will be any different this time.

It has reached the point where some players go as far as ignoring you. There was a time recently when we were staying in the same hotel as the other side. On the second morning of the match I strolled into the hotel reception and nodded a greeting to one of the opposing players. I was all set to have a chat about the prospects for play and so on when he just turned his back on me.

Once at Scarborough, I nipped out to post a letter and on my way back to the hotel, passed one of the opposition players walking in the opposite direction. Again, I made eye contact and started to speak – only for the player to walk straight past me as if I didn't exist. What an attitude! Surely we can be as aggressive as we like out in the middle but still behave like civilised human beings away from the action. We're all professional cricketers, for heaven's sake.

You can have as much needle as you want between 11 a.m. and 6.30 p.m., but just because you trade Anglo-Saxon insults in the heat of the moment, you don't continue to regard your opponent as a first-class prat when the dust settles. Sadly, though, there are too many young players around these days who seem to think it's fashionable to bear grudges.

I tell you this. If I'd kept a hit list of all the players I've had a spat with over the last 15 years, I would have filled a whole library of little black books. Instead I prefer to treat my fellow professionals with the respect they deserve, making me a member of an ever-dwindling minority who feel the same way. And that's a shame.

HAMPSHIRE V YORKSHIRE, BASINGSTOKE

Wednesday, 9 June. To Basingstoke for Championship and
National League games against Hampshire. And a reunion with
Peter Hartley. Jack, as he is known to his former Yorkshire team-
mates, was controversially released by the county at the end of
the 1997 season, clearing the decks for the emerging fast bowling
brigade. Hampshire wasted no time in snapping him up and at 39,
he is still doing the business.

Yorkshire released Jack too soon. I thought so at the time and I still
think so today. He was still an extremely useful bowler and an asset to
the team off the field, too. Although we had the current clutch of good
young fast bowlers coming into the side and urgently needing first-
team experience, Jack would have been very useful to have around in
one-day cricket and as cover in the first team. He would even have
made a smashing second team captain. I've always said you can't put
old heads on young shoulders and there were times last season when
our seam attack was crying out for someone like Jack. This season too,
for that matter. When he was released he still had a bit left in the tank
– as he proved at Hampshire last year by playing in 12 Championship
games and taking 31 wickets. And he's made a decent start this time
too.

He was treated in a pretty shoddy manner. He'd carried the
Yorkshire attack for five or six years and there were times when we had
to wheel him out three-quarters fit because there simply wasn't anyone

else. And he responded by running in as hard as ever. In ten years as a capped player, he worked his bollocks off for Yorkshire cricket and in 1997, even though he only played in eight Championship games, he topped our bowling averages with 23 wickets at 22.21.

Then suddenly, because there were a few young bowlers on the horizon, he was ditched. It was a hell of a shock for Jack – and everyone else, for that matter. The skipper had wanted to keep him on and said so publicly. I don't know the exact ins-and-outs but it seems cash was a bit tight, a player had to go and it was the old pro who got the chop.

Still, I'll always have happy memories of Jack on and off the field. Like a lot of ageing fast bowlers, he has suffered from the ravages of time because fast bowling is bloody hard work, believe me. It puts a lot of pressure on the ankles, the knees, the back, the shoulder. Everywhere. Running in 20 or 30 yards to bowl six balls an over 25 or 30 times a day is no party – particularly when you are quite likely to have to get up the next morning and start all over again.

In fact, I have known a lot of pacemen who say a silent vote of thanks for the painkillers and anti-inflammatories that get them out on to the pitch in a morning, wicketkeepers, too. But I dread to think what the long-term consequences might be. A painkiller is exactly what the name suggests and it isn't designed to cure the original damage.

Jack and I both came into the Yorkshire side together and I suppose you could say that at one stage we were like blood brothers. We roomed together for years and we received our county caps on the same day at Scarborough in 1987. And, as with Goughie, Gavin and the rest, I was behind the stumps for most of his Yorkshire career.

So I know better than anyone else how good a bowler he is. Far worse performers have picked up England caps but Jack has never been fashionable. Even so, in his prime he should undoubtedly have been given a Test opportunity as the so-called Headingley specialist and I'm certain he would have taken his share of wickets. He consistently puts the ball in the right areas, moves it away from the bat and, despite giving an impression to the contrary, he'll bowl all day for you. He can bat a bit, too.

Like a lot of quickies, Jack likes to convey the idea that as far as he's concerned, fast bowling is a 22 carat pain in the ass and he could find a million better ways to earn a living than slugging it out over 22 yards with unco-operative batsmen. Particularly if there happens to be a golf course in the immediate vicinity.

When we roomed together, he had the same early-morning routine every day. After somehow persuading his aching back to propel him out of bed, he'd stagger over to the window and take a peep through the curtains. If it was raining, he'd beam the broadest smile you're likely to see at 7 a.m. and trundle back into bed for another hour. If the sun was shining and he happened to be in a reasonable mood he might just condescend to put the kettle on. The pre-match warm-up was never a bed of roses and, like most senior members of the fast bowlers' union, he preferred his skipper to win the toss and bat. If not, when the captain asked what sort of field he'd like, he'd reply, 'A fucking great big one!'

Golf was, and still is, his passion. With a handicap of four, he's just about the best golfer on the county circuit and as a youngster he was good enough to be given a chance as an assistant pro at Keighley Golf Club. In the end, cricket provided a marginally more secure option but wherever Jack goes, the clubs go too. If there's any danger of play ending early for the day, he'll be on the phone to the local club, asking if he can fit in nine holes.

One year at the Scarborough Festival, working on the basis that after a long, hard season his services would not be required for a relatively meaningless friendly, he booked himself a tee-time down the road at his beloved Ganton. He was planning an early morning flier down the A64 when the awful news arrived that he was in the side at North Marine Road. I can safely report that the ball wasn't exactly thundering into the gloves on that occasion.

A character, Jack – a good lad and a good bowler. I once read an interview in one of the cricket magazines in which he said that if, in years to come, he is remembered as a bloody good county pro, he'd have no complaints. Fair enough. But in my book, he'll always be a better player than that.

PPP Healthcare County Championship, Basingstoke. 9–12 June. Yorkshire 192 (P.J. Hartley 8–65) and 141–3 (D. Byas 95) beat Hampshire 206 (C. Silverwood 5–43) and 124 (M. Hoggard 4–45, G.M. Hamilton 3–22) by 7 wickets.

CGU National League, Basingstoke. 13 June. Yorkshire Phoenix 191–9 (A. McGrath 75) beat Hampshire Hawks 164 (M.P. Vaughan 4–31) by 27 runs.

Hartley responded to the visit of his old colleagues with match figures of 11 for 113, including a first innings haul of 8 for 65. Afterwards he politely informed the watching Chairman of Selectors David Graveney that he didn't wish to be considered for the first Test against New Zealand at Edgbaston on 1 July. Despite his heroics, though, two more wins for Yorkshire and with a third of the season behind them they have moved up into third place in the County Championship and lead the National League Division One table with a 100 per cent record from five games. With a home game against Sussex in the Championship due to start on Tuesday followed by their sixth National League tussle, this time against Essex, confidence is running high.

The Championship win was a personal triumph for the captain. With the scores almost level on first innings, we needed someone to take control and make a winning score. A total of 130 doesn't sound a lot but on that pitch it was never going to be easy, particularly with Jack right bang in the groove. Dave led from the front, played some stunning strokes and we got home with plenty to spare.

It was the same on the Sunday. We looked to be in big trouble on 43 for 5 after 15 overs but this time it was Anthony McGrath who dug us out of a hole with another half century and we finished with 191, more than enough for our pace attack in the end. When you think

Mags wasn't even in the first-choice eleven at the start of the season, he's more than proved a point with a Championship century to his credit and a string of valuable knocks. He won't be the man to go if and when Dick Harden is recalled and at this rate a county cap can't be far away. I'm pleased for him.

The encouraging factor is that we are winning games without playing anywhere near to our potential. Apart from Mags and Bingo (not even Byas himself knows why he has been saddled with that nickname since he first broke into the side in 1986), the batsmen haven't really got going. Vaughan hit those two hundreds down at Chelmsford but he hasn't done much else and while most of us have chipped in – I collected another useful 50 in this game – we haven't looked convincing as a unit.

And, of course, the overseas man just isn't firing at all yet. When Greg does – and mark my words, he will – we'll really start to post some big scores. As it is, we've been hanging in long enough to give our bowlers the chance to win four of our seven games so far. And with a Headingley match against Sussex coming up followed by the return National League game against Essex on Saturday, we have a great chance to consolidate. Things are looking good.

I wish I could say I was as happy about the facilities at Basingstoke, though. I've already made my views clear about some of our own outgrounds but none of them can touch Basingstoke. Fourteen players, complete with a mountain of cricket gear, trying to fit into a dressing-room that's about the size of a decent garden shed doesn't work out. We sometimes refer to the dressing-room as the den or the pit but our comments about this particular venue were even less complimentary. And while we had a good laugh at the sight of players from both sides queuing up with the punters for a pee during the intervals, it's not something to raise the image of our game as we approach the closing stages of the World Cup. Players involved in a match between two of the top sides in the country have a right to expect something better.

Having said that, the toilet facilities were a million miles away from the captain's mind when he returned to the dressing-room after his match-winning knock. Guinness was his thought for the day and he promptly headed off to the hospitality tent for a couple of social pints. Bingo has always been fond of the black stuff and he's never been reluctant to celebrate a good win. So with a day and a half to spare before the National League game, there was obviously a bit of licence for us all. And why not? Work hard, play hard has always been our ethos and the skipper wasn't in any mood to argue.

After the game we all went our separate ways and agreed to reconvene in the hotel bar at 7 p.m. When we arrived it was pretty obvious that Dave had been in there all afternoon. He was really ticking. So we cordially invited him to share a night out with the lads and he graciously accepted. He's good company, the captain. He's never a man to show much emotion out in the middle but off duty he'll have a good time with the best of them. And I would never entirely rule him out of contention in the Phantom Sock-Snipper stakes.

When he's had a few pints, he likes nothing better than to recount his favourite tales although as the Guinness takes its toll, he starts to mumble a bit. Most of the lads have been around a while and they've heard his stories anyway. So they know to just let him ramble on and then when he starts to guffaw at the punchline, we join in and have a good laugh, too.

On this particular night, we were accompanied by Shaun Udal, the Hampshire spinner, and it wasn't long before he was cornered by Bingo. After a while he managed to break free to go to the toilet. On the way back, he came across to me. 'It's the captain, Dick. I can't understand a bloody word he's saying.'

As I say, I've been through the same routine a few times myself. So I was able to tell Shaun to just play him along, wait for the laugh and then chime in at full volume. Sure enough, that's exactly what he did – to the unconcealed delight of the watching Yorkshire players, who had seen it all before. Needless to say, Udal ended up on the receiving end of a few more incomprehensible stories for his pains.

After disposing of the best part of a barrel of Guinness, and I suspect a few chasers secretly added by one or two of the younger generation, the captain was eventually obliged to declare his innings closed and leave the proceedings early. He departed with a definite sway in the middle of the evening, not to be seen again until the following teatime.

His performance reminded me of another occasion on a pre-season tour in South Africa. Halfway through the tour we had a party night with the usual silly games and, on this occasion, a Karaoke competition. It was judged by three members of the Press, Rob Mills of the *Yorkshire Post*, David Warner, *Bradford Telegraph and Argus*, and Yorkshire Television's John Shires. Some people call these occasions male bonding; I prefer to think of it as a damn good night out. Anyway, Byas was paired with Chris Hassall, Yorkshire's chief executive. And for some reason, and I can't exactly recall why, they ended their command performance in breathtaking style, with the Chief balanced precariously on Bingo's shoulders.

Now Byas, or Gadget as we sometimes call him, is 6ft 4in and the Chief no more than 5ft 4in with his platforms on. So you can well imagine that the sight of Byas teetering around with Yorkshire's top man aboard was hilarious . . . for everyone except Hassall, of course. To his credit, he survived the equivalent of Becher's Brook and the Canal Turn in one piece and played his part to perfection. But I suspect he's steered clear of the captain at social events ever since.

Much to the disgust of Yorkshire's answer to Batman and Robin, the judges awarded the first prize to Michael Bevan, who never entered any competition without signalling his intention to win, and Paul Grayson, who subsequently decided the safest way to avoid nights like this was to jump ship and join Essex. But there was a consolation prize for Byas and the Chief for their impersonation of the Leaning Tower of Pisa.

I was on the receiving end of a Byas prank at our Christmas bash a couple of years ago. He's always been a man for formalities but I thought it was a bit over the top when I received a printed invitation to attend the players' annual party at a hotel in York – formal dress. Now I've no problem about donning the old dinner jacket but I though the captain was going a bit far this time and rang him up to say so. I pointed out that it was an informal function strictly for the lads and the last thing we wanted was to be cooped up in a DJ. I also said that some of the younger players would be less than thrilled at shelling out the best part of a hundred quid for all the gear.

At first, Bingo adopted his stubborn farmer's stance and refused to change but eventually I had a call saying that on reflection I was probably right – and why not make it a fancy dress do instead? As it was York, we settled on Viking costumes. Brilliant.

I bought myself a blond wig, begged, borrowed or stole a furry waistcoat and some leather gaiters and persuaded my dad to lend me his old Jesus sandals. When I looked in the mirror before setting off, a pretty good replica of Erik the Viking stared back at me. I put my day clothes in the boot and set off with every prospect of a good night on the immediate horizon. I didn't smell a rat until the commissionaire on the door said, 'Good evening, Mr Blakey. We've been expecting you.' Now we like our cricket in Yorkshire and it's not a complete surprise for players to be recognised in the street or when we're out socially, but not dressed up as a Viking warrior. Sure enough, the only man in fancy dress was Richard John Blakey. And nobody enjoyed it more than the captain, who had a pint of lager waiting for me as I strode into the function room.

To make matters worse, there were three other groups having their Christmas party in the same room – and the waiters and waitresses were in costumes not a million miles away from my own Viking number. So every time I nipped out to the bar or to go to the toilet, I was assailed by the other guests, asking me for a bottle of plonk or another round of drinks. I took it all in good part, of course, and it will always be remembered as a damn good night.

YORKSHIRE V SUSSEX, HEADINGLEY

Tuesday, 15 June. After 12 innings Greg Blewett, Yorkshire's 1999 overseas player, is still waiting for his first Championship century. He has scored just 272 runs at an average of 20.92. Last year, his fellow South Australian Darren Lehmann, a member of Australia's World Cup squad, hit 969 runs in 16 innings, averaging 60.56. Yorkshire deny Blewett's form has reached crisis point but he desperately needs a big score against Sussex. He is Yorkshire's fifth import since 129 years of Home Rule were abandoned in 1992. Blakey has played alongside them all.

Inevitably, there are one or two whispers that Blewie should be dropped. But not in the Yorkshire dressing-room. The players are 100 per cent behind him. He has a proven track record at the highest level with three Test centuries against England and some sensational innings on the last Ashes tour to Australia. He's scored a mountain of runs in Sheffield Shield cricket, he's a quality player and we know he will come good eventually.

Having said that, his form has been a bitter disappointment for everyone – not least Blewett himself. He's a good guy and he's fitted into the set-up as well as, if not better than, any of the other overseas players we've had – Sachin Tendulkar, Richie Richardson, Michael Bevan and Darren Lehmann. With the possible exception of Lehmann. I'll be talking about all our overseas men in a moment but Lehmann was a near-impossible act to follow in the dressing-room and Greg has just about achieved it.

When he first arrived, fresh from Australia's tour to the West Indies, he looked in fantastic nick in the nets. He had made an incredible 1,175 runs at an average of 146.86 in the first half of the Australian season, hitting a double century and five hundreds. So not surprisingly I was convinced he would score heavily from day one, but it hasn't happened. Playing on Headingley pitches that have been doing a bit hasn't helped and when he ran into a decent track down at Chelmsford, he started to show how good he was. But in the second innings a ball got through his visor and re-arranged his teeth. It wasn't enough to stop him resuming his innings after a visit to the dentist but it can't have helped his confidence.

And he's had a couple of dodgy lbw decisions. In fact, he's been out leg before a few times, hit on the front pad taking a big step forward. He would probably have got away with it in Australia but over here the umpires tend to give those. That's something he'll need to adapt.

And he will. He's netting at every available opportunity and working very hard with Martyn Moxon. Significantly, he hasn't let his bad trot get to him. These Aussies are tough cookies and he isn't going to give this away. But like any batsman having a poor run, the doubts will be creeping in and he needs a score. Having said that, while it's important for the overseas batsman to score runs, I believe we have a strong enough batting line-up to cover for him while he's out of sorts.

As a team-mate, there's not a lot you can do other than keep on encouraging Blewie. If someone like Chalkie or Bingo came and asked me if I could spot any blemishes in their technique, I could do it straight away. We've grown up in the same side together and I know their game almost as well as my own. But I'd never seen Greg play until he joined us at the start of the season. I don't know how he plays when he's in prime form so I can't possibly try to put him right when he's struggling.

But as far as I'm concerned, leaving him out isn't an option. He's a more than useful seam bowler, his fielding is brilliant and his input on and off the field is excellent. His presence in the side is important because leaving out your overseas man gives all the wrong vibes to the opposition. I'm sure that by the end of the season, this bad start will be history and he will have played several very big and very important innings for us. And the sooner he starts, the better.

As I mentioned earlier, he's our fifth foreigner, although when I first came into the side in 1985 Yorkshire were still the only county not to employ an overseas player. The players felt they were working with one hand tied behind their backs. If every other county had a world-class overseas player in their line-up what chance did we have? We wanted a level playing field. A lot of anguish built up in the dressing-room over the years because everywhere we went there was someone like Malcolm Marshall, Courtney Walsh, Curtly Ambrose, Waqar Younis or Allan Donald waiting for us.

And if it wasn't a world-class quickie, people like Viv Richards were looking to fill their boots against the only county side without an overseas player to return fire. We had some useful players, don't get me wrong, but no one in that league. It was like canons against peashooters. We were trying our best but just kept getting rolled over. The players were very disillusioned about it. There was a lot of negative thinking and looking back there were games when we were beaten before a ball was bowled. As a young player it was no good to me to hear experienced pros take one look at Marshall steaming in and say, 'How the fuck are we going to get any runs against him?' It wasn't a healthy environment and thankfully it's completely different now. We let the opposition worry about us.

David Bairstow and Phil Carrick were my first two captains and they both felt particularly strongly about it. They were supported by the senior players although at first I was content to take a backseat. As an 18 year-old trying to make my way in the game, I already had enough on my plate. But Carrick, Bairstow and the others were constantly kicking up a fuss about it with the committee, and as far as the players were concerned it was only a matter of time before the club abandoned over a hundred years of history and brought in a foreign player. Eventually, the pressure from the players paid off – particularly after Sir Lawrence Byford took over as president and chairman in 1991. Among other things, he saw the marketing potential in Yorkshire's first high-profile overseas player and jumped aboard the bandwagon.

And that first signing couldn't have been a much bigger name. When Yorkshire announced that summer that they were finally going to join the overseas party their choice was Craig McDermott, the Australian fast bowler rated number one in the world. His signing created tremendous interest throughout the game and above all in the dressing-room. The days of turning the other cheek would be over at last.

So it was a hell of a blow, to put it mildly, when we learned on our pre-season tour of South Africa the following year that McDermott had pulled out because of injury. Yorkshire had to move fast to find a replacement. And instead of the best fast bowler in the world they came up with potentially the greatest batsman around, Sachin Tendulkar.

He was only 18 but already had an enormous reputation. He had played in eleven Tests for India and scored one century and four fifties. He met the Yorkshire players in our first match of the season against Surrey at The Oval. We were all in suits and ties for the photocall – it was still very much formal dress in those days – and he strolled in wearing jeans. Mind you he could dress as smartly as the next man if he had to and if he was worried about being Yorkshire's first overseas player it never showed. I suppose at that age, you just take life as it comes.

As a batsman he really was a class act and by the time he finishes he will probably be Test cricket's leading run-maker. Yet it was always asking a lot for someone of his age and inexperience to walk in to such a high-profile role and in the end he didn't make the volume of runs expected of him.

He had a bit of trouble coping with lateral movement and had to wait until late in the season before he scored his maiden century for us against Durham. But he played some marvellous innings and batting with him was an experience in itself. Having him around made a big difference. Where, in the past, two of us batting in tandem might have been finding it hard going against the other side's overseas man, Sachin was happy to take the responsibility. He didn't have an enormous amount of tactical input but that was understandable for someone of his age and experience. It was fascinating, though, to hear him talk about playing the spinners – a different world.

And Sachin was very popular with the lads. I'm sometimes asked if there was a bit of resentment in the dressing-room over a young kid coming in with a big reputation and a salary to match. But I can honestly say there was none of that. None at all. I have always believed that if a player can earn big money out of this game, then good luck to him. And I'm sure that's how the rest of the players felt about Sachin.

His arrival created a lot of interest, raised the profile of the club and did nothing but good for the image of Yorkshire cricket.

He was a bit shy and reserved at first. But he was lucky that Vinod Kambli, who played with him in Bombay and later for India, was doing a professional stint in the Bradford League and was around to provide a familiar face. He played himself quietly into the dressing-room routine but by the time we'd finished with him he was knocking back the Baileys on ice and proving himself a real party animal.

And he loved the dressing-room antics, too. Never more so than The Day Robbo Went Missing. We were playing Durham up at the Durham University ground and after bowling Durham out fairly cheaply, we finished the first day with Martyn Moxon and Simon Kellett also back in the pavilion. Mark Robinson, our fast bowler who now plays for Sussex, woke up on the second morning feeling a bit queasy and after our warm-up decided to stroll into town and buy some tablets from Boots. Simon agreed to join him.

Now Robbo has always has been a professional number eleven so it was reasonable for him to assume that he would not be required to strap on the pads before lunch. So after visiting Boots, he decided to have a look around Durham city centre. Unfortunately, back at the cricket ground, things were not going to plan. Wickets were tumbling and when Peter Hartley went out to bat at number nine, Robbo's absence was noted. Panic stations.

Doug Padgett was our coach then and he and Wayne Morton, the physio, leaped into their cars and set off in search of our number eleven. Now Durham city centre is a combination of one-way system and traffic-free zone so Wayne had to abandon his car and go chasing around the cobbled streets looking for a tall, dark-haired man in a Yorkshire tracksuit. By a pure miracle, he spotted Mark coming out of a fruit shop armed with a bag of peaches. 'Robbo, you're in next,' bellowed Morton. Robinson, assuming he was being wound up, grinned cheerfully in reply until the awful truth dawned on him. As it was easier to reach the ground on foot, he set off at top speed, noting as he approached that the scoreboard read 101 for 9.

By the time he arrived, with a bag of peaches in one hand and a Boots carrier in the other, his team-mates had been divided into two groups. The first party whipped off his tracksuit and put on his whites. Then the second group took over, hastily transforming Robbo into something vaguely resembling a batsman. I recall breaking off at one point and seeing Sachin rolling around the dressing-room bench, helpless with laughter. Tears were streaming down his face. He'd never seen anything like this before. Neither had I for that matter. To crown the story, Robbo went out and recorded one of his rare big scores, four not out. And by the time Sachin batted in the second innings, he had recovered well enough to score his only century for the county. We won by five wickets.

With him around on the circuit we were never short of a top-class Indian meal. Everywhere we went, the local Indian restaurant would invite Sachin and the rest of the boys round and there was never any question of paying. All they wanted was a picture of Sachin with the staff. And at one restaurant in Darlington during that same Durham game, he ended up surrounded by about forty waiters all trying to get in on the Polaroid picture. It will still be on the wall at the end of the next millennium, I suppose. He made a big impression with the members, too, and has always said he'd love to come back to Yorkshire one day. If he does, I fancy he'll score more than the 1,070 first-class runs he managed first time around. But as far as his overall impact in that 1992 season is concerned, the bottom line is that he didn't score the runs we needed.

The same criticism could be levelled at his successor, Richard Benjamin Richardson. Like Tendulkar, Richie arrived in Yorkshire as one of the best batsmen in the world; in fact I think he was rated at number one at the start of the 1993 season, his first with us. But he also struggled to come to terms with the conditions over here. He was a back-foot player and found it hard work against bowling of fuller length on pitches that moved around.

Unlike Sachin, though, there was no question of Richie Rich taking a back seat. From day one, Richie had an aura about him. He was a great character in the dressing-room and tremendous at motivating the other players. As far as he was concerned, Yorkshire were unbeatable. And even if his performances over two seasons didn't live up to his own or anyone else's expectations, Yorkshire and English cricket owes him a huge debt: Darren Gough.

Goughie was just breaking into the side when Richie arrived and as captain of the West Indies he knew a thing or two about fast bowlers. He spotted gold in Goughie straight away and more or less took him under his wing. He gave Darren the confidence and self-belief he needed at that stage of his career and was always there encouraging him in the early days.

Richie believed totally in his own ability to set the world on fire and, to be fair to him, he had done just that at Test level. And he passed that self-confidence on to Goughie and some of the other young players coming through. He convinced Darren that he was capable of going all the way at a time when he might have been having one or two doubts about his future. And Goughie is the first person to acknowledge the debt he owes to Richie.

From a team point of view Richie, like Sachin, simply didn't get enough runs, though, and in the end he left halfway through his second season suffering from fatigue. The previous year he had been forced to interrupt his season when his mother died. Then his little boy had a nasty accident involving a car and was rushed to hospital critically ill. So Richie had to dash home again, although thankfully the little fellow made a full recovery. On top of those worries was the huge amount of high-powered international cricket he had been playing virtually without a break. He was under pressure to perform for the West Indies and for us all the time and in the end he was exhausted. But he played some tremendous innings for us, particularly against Warwickshire at Edgbaston in 1993.

In the first innings we had to go through the usual routine of waking him up to go into bat at the fall of the first wicket. As I recall, it was Yorkshire Day. So he had attached a big white rose to his cap and he walked out to do battle with Allan Donald, then as now one of the fastest bowlers in the world. The white rose was like a red rag to a bull to Donald as Richie strolled out to the middle. He didn't last long. Donald bounced him, Richie hooked and Paul Smith at deep fine leg took the catch.

Second innings – wake up Richie, you're in. Same process. He dusted himself down, put on the cap with the big white rose, picked up his bat and ambled out to cross swords with Donald once more. It was probably the most amazing contest I have seen. Donald was really fired up and came steaming in as fast as he's ever bowled. And there was Richie at the other end; no helmet, a white flower in his cap. It was one of those days when the whole ground senses something special is about to happen. And it did.

Donald bounced it, Richie hooked. Four. Donald bounced him again, Richie hooked. Donald sent three men out. One just in front of square and two others waiting for the hook. And Richie just took them on. You know the cricket is special when all the players are on the balcony and, make no mistake, everyone was out to watch this. For twenty minutes or half an hour it was incredible stuff. And Richie won the duel. He saw off Donald and scored a hundred, his only century for Yorkshire.

On another occasion he was facing Courtney Walsh, his West Indies team-mate. And he relished that challenge there as well. He couldn't really be doing with someone bowling little English seamers at him on a county outground. But give him the big stage and a world-class opponent and he could be devastating. Tactically he was never quite the big influence you might expect from the captain of the West Indies. But you certainly knew he'd stood in the slips with the quicks on the rampage. 'Make him smell the ball, man!' he'd shout at Goughie. Or 'Take him to Doomsbridge!'

One of the best Richie Rich stories happened down at Maidstone. He was fielding in the covers to start with but when he was switched to gully, he started shouting all his usual encouragement to the bowler. Then he looked down and saw a pile of dog dirt three feet in front of him. The bowler started his run-up but Richie stopped the game. He went over to the umpire, Jack Bond, and said, 'We can't carry on, Jack, there's some dog deposit on the ground. Come over here and have a look.'

Now Jack's been around a long time but this was obviously a one-off. He'd no idea what to do. All he could say was, 'The dog's gone, Richie, there's nothing I can do.' Richie wasn't impressed. I can't imagine what all this looked like to the crowd but the players were in hysterics. Richie sorted it himself in the end, running down to the fine leg boundary, tearing some branches off a tree and covering the offending pile with leaves. Play resumed but needless to say three balls later, Richie was faced with a diving stop he just didn't fancy and the ball flew to the third man boundary.

Away from the action he was a great guy as well – the coolest dude in Yorkshire. He had a pair of Oakley sunglasses and I reckon he used to wear them 24 hours a day. He'd arrive at the ground in them, play in them, wear them in the pub afterwards. And I swear I once saw him driving home late at night, headlights on, it's pitch black and he's still wearing the Oakleys. He played a mean electric guitar, too. A good man! But cricket-wise he never made the impact we hoped for.

And then along came Bevan. Not many people had even heard of Michael Bevan when he arrived at Headingley at the start of the 1995 season. He'd just broken into the Australian side after years of heavy scoring in Sheffield Shield cricket for New South Wales and I believe he was recommended to Yorkshire by Peter Philpott, the spin bowling coach who had worked with us off and on for a few years. But apart from a couple of seasons with Rawtenstall in the Lancashire League, Bev was a totally unknown quantity over here. Not for long. From day one, this guy was on a different planet.

He had the classic tough Australian mentality. He'd been brought up in a hard school and his will to win was 120 per cent. With Bevan around, fielding drills became a whole new ball game. I'd be the first to admit that before the 1995 season, fielding practice was a fairly light-hearted routine and there were times when we just went through the motions. Not any more. Michael took over the sessions and woe betide anyone who didn't give it their all. His bollockings were legendary – and not just directed at the younger players. It was a bit of an eye opener, to say the least. As the overseas player, he saw it as part of his job to run the fielding practices and Martyn Moxon, who was captain, didn't have any problem with that. He wanted the overseas man to have more influence and by and large we accepted that Bevan was bringing a new dimension to our game that would improve our chances in the long run.

The trouble with Bev was that his way always had to be the right way. For me, if someone is putting in 100 per cent at practice, then fair enough. But with Bevan, if you weren't doing it his way, you weren't doing it properly. That rankled with a lot of the players. We needed his aggression and we needed his input but as time went by, one or two of the players inevitably started to bridle at his attitude. 'Who the hell does he think he is?' You'll get the picture.

The only man to really take him on, though, was Peter Hartley. It was back in the 1995 season at Scarborough and Bev was taking the fielding practice as usual, hitting huge high catches. The fielders were expected to go for everything as if it was a Lord's final. As it happened Jack was nearing the end of a long, hard season in which he ended up bowling nearly 500 overs and taking 71 wickets at 21.91 apiece. And at 35, he was no spring chicken.

As this was the morning after a hard day, the old back was a bit stiff. So when his catch went up, he didn't put in quite the amount of effort that Bev demanded. The catch inevitably fell short as Jack's gallop slowed down into a canter and then a gentle trot. As usual, Bevan let go with the verbals, letting Jack know in no uncertain terms what he thought of his approach to fielding drills. Jack just gave him a long, hard stare, shrugged and said, 'Bollocks to this, I'm off for a cup of tea.' Michael couldn't believe it. He was furious and chased him around the square twice before Jack made it safely back to the pavilion. They didn't speak to one another for days. We still talk about it now. But nowadays if one player has a go at another, rightly or wrongly, they shake hands and forget it just as quickly. Instead, the bad blood lived on between these two.

As a player, Bev did it his way, too. It would be hugely unfair to describe him as a selfish cricketer because everything he did was always in the best interests of the team. Perhaps self-centred would be a better description. He had an insatiable appetite for runs and he simply would not give his wicket away, particularly in the one-day game. It's no surprise to me that he has gone on to become one of the best one-day players in the world. In a run chase, he always backed himself to win the game. While he was at the crease he believed victory was never beyond us. And he felt that if he was batting at the end, Yorkshire would win.

His attitude was a million miles away from Richie, who would go in, smash a quick 50 and then get out, leaving the lower order with a job to do. Not Bevan. He assumed responsibility from the moment he arrived at the crease and took it upon himself to win the game. He had an uncanny instinct for finding the gaps. He knew where he was going to put the ball before the bowler began his run-up. And that's exactly what he did. A tremendous skill. He could accumulate eight or ten runs an over without hitting a boundary. And in one-day cricket he was wonderful to bat with because he simply never panicked.

He was an incredible influence in the field, too. He was a marvellous athlete and he could really cover the ground. But inevitably, he expected the same high standards from everyone and if he thought someone wasn't putting everything in, he would think nothing of yelling at them for more effort.

He was even harder on himself, though. When he got out, either for a duck or a hundred, he'd come back into the dressing-room, hurl the bat around and let go with every expletive in the business – and a few more on top. It reached the point where a couple of the lads used to nip down as Bev was making his way back to the pavilion and sit in a corner, counting the swear words. We'd get up to 30 or 40 before he calmed down. And then he'd start all over again – another 25 or 30. Whether that's the kind of example the overseas player should be setting to the younger generation is open to argument.

Some of his behaviour off the field left something to be desired, too. He did his best to avoid talking to the members which, like it or not, is very much part of a Yorkshire player's duty. And to say he was reluctant to sign autographs is putting it mildly. He would just walk straight past kids with books in their hands. Once at Scarborough, he put a sign up in the dressing-room window which read: No autographs until after the game. That's no way to behave.

So while I admired him tremendously as a cricketer, and I still do, his attitude towards his team-mates, the Yorkshire members and supporters at various times could be very poor. That was disappointing. And it no doubt counted against his chances of becoming captain for the 1996 season after Martyn had resigned. Apparently it was a straight choice between David Byas and Bevan but I'm sure there would have been problems in the dressing-room if Bevan had got the nod. The decision was taken during the winter so for the most part, the players were blissfully unaware about what was going on. But I think the vast majority of us would have backed David.

On balance, though, I have absolutely no doubt that Bevan's influence on Yorkshire cricket was good. He had been involved in successful sides in Australia and he showed us what was required to become a winning unit. The feeling was: If this is what it takes, let's get on with it. He was our first Australian and he brought a new dimension to our dressing-room. It's fair to say he was the catalyst for the improvement we have seen in Yorkshire cricket over the last few years. He made us sit up and realise everything has to be high quality – training, fielding, team talks, the lot. The days of mediocrity were no longer acceptable. In truth, we knew before he arrived that something drastic had to be done. Michael Bevan did it.

In his two years he set new standards and fully expected to return after touring with Australia in 1997. Instead his replacement, Darren Lehmann, was retained. I understand Bevan was angry about it because he believed there were assurances that he would be re-signed for 1998. But no one, least of all Michael, reckoned on the influence – on and off the field – of good time guy Lehmann.

Looking back, it's impossible to believe that Darren was in fact our third choice Aussie. When it became obvious that Bevan would be involved in the Ashes series, Yorkshire moved straight in for Michael Slater, his New South Wales colleague who had lost his place in the Test side. His signing was announced at the annual meeting in Leeds complete with a press release saying how keen Michael was to come and do the business for Yorkshire. Then the Aussies picked him as well, so we were down to the third man in the boat. Lehmann.

He missed the start of the 1997 season because of his commitments with South Australia and we were down south playing at Oxford University in a friendly when he arrived. Goughie had told us Lehmann enjoyed a McDonalds or three so when we knew he was on his way, we sent out for a takeaway – team McDonalds. Burgers, chips, milk shakes, the lot. Darren walked into the hotel, took one look at the fare on show and you could see him thinking, this lot will do for me. The first thing he did was buy a round of drinks. He was a totally chilled-out bloke and just sat straight down and chatted with the lads as if he'd known us all his life.

He soon revealed he could play a bit, too. He wasn't picked for our first Benson and Hedges game against Lancashire at Old Trafford so he put in some practice in the indoor school there. Word soon filtered back that the power of his hitting was awesome. In his first season he scored 1,575 runs at 63 and the following season, despite injury problems and an early finish to link up with the Australian squad, he totalled 969 at 60.56. Super figures, which speak for themselves. He could take attacks apart in the four-day game and he was a wonderful one-day performer too. And his tactical input was spot on. It was never a case of do it my way; just, hey, why don't we give this a try?

But it was his influence off the field that made him the best overseas player we have had and surely one of the best to appear in the English game. A completely different character from his predecessor. Where you could never quite be sure whether Bevan would blow hot or cold, depending on which side of bed he got out of in the morning, the new guy never changed from day one. It was as if he said to himself, 'Right, I'm Yorkshire's overseas player, I have a responsibility on and off the field and I will give it everything.' He never missed a chance to talk to the members and thought nothing of stopping for a chat with Sir Lawrence Byford, the club president, if he happened to be passing. He must have signed a million autographs; there was always a queue, he always obliged and it didn't end there. He usually had a chat or shared a joke with the people who had waited for his signature. And I don't think he turned down a single request from any branch of the media.

In the den, he was different class. If you speak to any of the lads they will talk about his comradeship as well as his tremendous ability as a player. Nothing was ever too much trouble. If you wanted a word about your game, he would sit and listen for hours and come up with some sound advice. And if any of the lads had problems off the field, he was always there to talk to. He could spot if one of us was having a difficult time on or off the field and would be there to help out.

Having said that, he wasn't afraid to hand out a bollocking if he thought anyone was out of line. But it's a lot easier to remember the piss-ups and the parties. Lehmann's philosophy was simple: work hard and then play hard. He did both – and if that's how a player wants to live, no problem, provided he does the business out in the middle. Darren always did. If we had won, he'd say, 'Right lads, let's go out and enjoy ourselves. The first round is on me.'

A couple of years ago, we were down in Devon for the first round of the NatWest Trophy and won it early on. As we were staying over that night, Lehmann organised a session in the bar which was in full swing when David Warner, one of the Yorkshire Press boys, came in. David was struggling with a serious dose of the flu and was trying to sneak in on the blind side for a mineral water to take up to his room. As soon as the Aussie spotted him, a pint appeared on the bar and poor old Plum found himself heavily involved in some ancient Aussie drinking ritual instead of tucking himself up for an early night. He felt even worse in the morning.

Darren would think nothing of taking all the lads out for a Chinese and picking up the tab. His home was open house in the barbecue season. And he had a marvellous knack of relieving tension in the dressing-room. If he spotted things were getting a bit heated he would summon up a perfectly-timed fart to lower the temperature a bit. Or he'd do one of his genital impressions – which I probably couldn't describe here even if the rules of decency permitted it. All our overseas players have had a lot going for them in one way or another but the bottom line is that Darren Lehmann was more or less perfect. I don't envy Greg having to follow him.

A lot of people claim, of course, that in an ideal world there would be no overseas players in the English game and I can see their point. But there are two sides to the argument. On the one hand, having high-class overseas players is a great opportunity for youngsters to go out and play against some of the top players in the world. Take Matthew Wood, who did tremendously well for us in his first full season last year. He was thrown in at the deep end against people who had heard his reputation and were doing their best to turn him over. He was tested with everything. They bowled fast and short and Wood stood his ground and came through it. He learned a lot in the process and if he goes on to play Test cricket he will know what to expect. On the other hand, for every top overseas player in our game, there is an Englishman missing out.

PPP Healthcare County Championship, Headingley. 15–18 June. Yorkshire 271 (M. Vaughan 71) and 157 lost to Sussex 192 and 239–5 (R. Montgomerie 110, C. Adams 58) by 5 wickets.

YORKSHIRE PHOENIX V ESSEX EAGLES, HEADINGLEY. CGU NATIONAL LEAGUE

Saturday, 19 June. After a three-day reverse against Sussex in the Championship, Yorkshire's hopes of bouncing straight back to winning ways and maintaining their 100 per cent record in the National League are shattered by Essex. A poor performance.

In a nutshell, a thoroughly crap week. We talked as a squad earlier in the season of the need to find a killer instinct, of turning match-winning opportunities into victories. Against Sussex, we had two chances and didn't take either of them. In the first innings we reached 220 for 5 and should have added at least another 120. Instead, we gave our wickets away and finished up with 270. Then, after our bowlers had put us back in charge with a lead of 79, which should have been more than enough at Headingley, we proceeded to bat even worse second time around. We showed a total lack of application and the way we gave our wickets away was criminal. Without Hamilton's unbeaten 30 we would have only just scraped past 100.

We should have batted them out of the game and set them a fourth innings target of around 350 or 400. Instead, it was 240 and the psychological advantage was with them. If they'd been set 375, they would never have got them in a million years. But 240 is a whole new ball game mentally and they won with something to spare.

We deserved to lose. Unless we can kill teams off when we establish what should be a winning position, we can forget about championships and trophies. There was a team meeting afterwards when David and Martyn spelt out exactly where we had let ourselves down. But we knew that anyway.

We've now lost four games, three in the Championship and one in the National League, and three of those defeats have been at Headingley. I wrote earlier of how we want to create a fortress for ourselves on our home ground; instead it has now been labelled a graveyard in some sections of the press. I don't go along with that because in the defeats by Middlesex and Sussex we have carved out a winning position only to chuck it away. After reducing Middlesex to 80 for 5 chasing 220, we should have won. We didn't, and now we have thrown away another victory against Sussex.

So instead of strengthening our position in the top three, we're heading for what could be a decisive phase of the season dreaming of what might have been. In the next three weeks or so, we have huge Championship games against Leicestershire, who are fourth, and Warwickshire, who are second. Both away. We also start our NatWest campaign down in Herefordshire on Wednesday and if we win that one we'll almost certainly meet Leicester again in the fourth round. Throw in a Super Cup quarter-final against Hampshire on Friday, hopefully a semi-final early in July and National League games against Leicester, Warwickshire and Gloucester and you'll see what I mean about a decisive period of the season.

And on top of last week's poor results, the injuries are starting to bite. Hutchison is still not ready to return after his back problem. He's had to re-model his action and is going to be out for a while longer. In the Sussex game, Goughie aggravated a calf strain he picked up in the World Cup and he's been ruled out for a month. He'll miss the first Test against New Zealand. Silverwood has been our best bowler but he had to miss the Sussex and Essex games with a knee injury and there's no certainty he'll be back for the NatWest tie or the Super Cup. And White was unable to bowl more than a handful of overs in Sussex's second innings because of a groin strain. Basically that leaves us with the three least experienced members of the pace attack, Hamilton, Hoggard and Sidebottom and heaven help us if any of them break down.

So testing times ahead. And one way or the other, by the time we travel to Scarborough for the game against Northants on 20 July, we'll know exactly whether we're serious contenders or not.

CGU National Cricket League, Headingley. 19 June. Yorkshire Phoenix 194 lost to Essex Eagles 241 (N. Hussain 114) by 47 runs.

AUSTRALIA V PAKISTAN, LORD'S. WORLD CUP FINAL

Sunday, 20 June. Away from the county circuit the World Cup – our so-called Carnival of Cricket, ends in victory for Australia, the favourites, over Pakistan in a disappointingly one-sided final.

On balance a good competition, and the best team won. The World Cup raised the profile of our game and, by and large, was well covered in the media. It started slowly on some early-season pitches and if anything, too many games were won too easily. For the most part, though, the World Cup captured the imagination of the sporting public and, at least for a while, kept football off the back pages of the tabloids. For the first time in years I've noticed kids out in the park playing cricket instead of football. I actually spotted a genuine case of 'I'm Klusener, you can be Warne!'

I wasn't totally happy about the second phase Super Sixes format and in the end it was only Australia's incredible victory over South Africa at Headingley, when Steve Waugh's century was one of the finest one-day innings ever played, that spared the organisers' blushes. If Australia had lost, Zimbabwe would have qualified for the last four instead of the eventual champions because of their record in the first phase – patently a nonsense.

Instead the Aussies beat South Africa again in a last-over semi-final victory that had the whole sporting nation riveted to their television screens and we all waited in eager anticipation of a thrilling final against Pakistan. But the Pakistanis never competed, Warne rolled them over and Yorkshire's very own Darren Lehmann was out there hitting the winning runs in mid-afternoon. Good news for Lehmann, a letdown for cricket.

But you have to admire the way the Aussies played it. They won seven games on the bounce to lift the cup which proves yet again that they simply never know when they are beaten. I've seen this mental toughness at first hand by playing alongside first Bevan and then Lehmann and until we acquire it in the English game we will never match them.

As it was, England's early exit was a disaster. You can argue until you're blue in the face about whether we picked the right players or not and with the great gift of hindsight we could all now sit down and pick a side that would have done better. Even so, the men chosen should have been good enough to qualify for the second phase. But they just didn't perform.

From a purely Yorkshire viewpoint, Goughie and Gavin Hamilton did well and can look back on their performances with pride. Darren is an established performer on the world stage and confirmed his place among the best fast bowlers in the game by finishing fifth in the bowling averages with 11 wickets from four games at 17 runs apiece. He rarely bowls poorly at any level and he was one of the few England players to come out of the competition with credit.

As I expected, Gav emerged as potentially a world-class all-rounder. He will be a bit disappointed with his bowling but for a Scotland player to take on some of the best bowlers in the world and finish tenth in the final averages is a magnificent achievement. He scored runs against both Australia and Pakistan to finish with 217 from five innings at an average of 54.25. Those figures were good enough to place him above world-class performers like Ganguly, Bevan, Tendulkar and Mark Waugh and surely he will be in the England selectors' thoughts now.

Changes are obviously afoot following our failure. David Lloyd's term as coach is over and it's an open secret that Alec Stewart will lose the captaincy, too. I feel sorry for them both. I've always liked Lloyd and if everyone had worked as hard as he has, the England team would be in better shape right now.

And to sack Stewart is grossly unfair. It strikes me that the powers-that-be are looking for a scapegoat for our one-day World Cup failure and the easy way out is to dismiss Alec for the five-day Test series against New Zealand. New coach, new captain, new start. We've heard it all before – but less than 12 months ago, don't forget, Stewart led England to a series victory over South Africa.

I've a lot of time for Alec – and not just because he's a member of the wicketkeepers' union. He's given everything for England down the years in any number of roles – opening batsman, middle order batsman, wicketkeeper-batsman, captain. And finally the whole lot. People keep telling me that to be captain, opening bat and wicketkeeper at Test level is an impossible job. Is it? Alec Stewart has shown it can be done and he has that series win over South Africa to prove it. Having said that, of course, the triple role places an almost intolerable burden on the individual involved, even someone as focused as Alec.

So who takes over? Essex captain Nasser Hussain is the front-runner but it won't surprise anyone that my choice would be David Byas. He's had one or two mentions and I read an article saying that if England are looking for someone who won't be afraid to knock a few heads together, then Byas is their man. Too right!

Dave made his Yorkshire début a year after me and we've grown up in the side together. And I can honestly say it's been a privilege to play alongside him. He is the straightest bloke I know and in my book that counts for a lot in a captain. If he has something to say to a player, good or bad, he says it to his face. There's no talking behind anyone's back, no whispers to the media, no back-stabbing. With Bingo, what you see is what you get.

He gives 200 per cent for the team and all he asks is that his players show the same level of commitment. As a captain, he has matured a lot since he succeeded Martyn Moxon in 1996. He responds well to different situations, he's tactically sound, he's prepared to listen and the players respond to him. But above all he isn't afraid to take responsibility and if he gets it wrong he won't blame anyone else. I haven't seen much of him in action with the media but the Press boys I have talked to speak highly of his straightforward, honest approach. And, as I have said before, he is more than capable of holding down a place as a batsman.

Hussain is the favourite, though. And I would have no problems with his appointment. Apart from one A tour in 1990 I have had very few dealings with him off the field. But he's a talented, dangerous attacking batsman who is clearly worth his place in the side. He's an aggressive cricketer with an abrasive, in-your-face approach that isn't everyone's cup of tea. He's been involved in a bit of needle with the Yorkshire players down the years but that doesn't worry me. Indeed, by all accounts, England could do with more aggression and if Hussain can provide it, all well and good.

But whoever gets the nod, it is absolutely vital that he is given overall responsibility and above all the final say on the field and in team selection. Give him a coach, by all means, but the coach should be there as his right-hand man, not the team leader. Here at Yorkshire, we have David as captain with Martyn as coach. Byas takes the big decisions but he knows he has Frog, as Martyn has always been called, to call on if he needs any guidance or someone to take away some of the hassle. For his part, Moxon organises the nets and practice sessions, works with the players on an individual basis and has overall responsibility for the way things are run off the field. His official title is Director of Cricket and he's in overall control of the cricketing side of the club's affairs from the first eleven downwards. The pair have always got on well and the system works. There is no reason why England cannot have a similar set-up.

To an outsider, though – and remember I haven't been directly involved with the England squad for six years so I'm not privy to all the innermost secrets of the dressing-room these days – there are too many chiefs and not enough Indians; too many men in blazers. Take a look at the England balcony in the middle of a Test match and there seem to be all sorts of people milling about who, on the face of it, have nothing to do with the cricket being played out in the middle.

I'm not privileged to know how the England and Wales Cricket Board operates and I'm sure all the administrative staff have a role to perform within the organisation. But that role does not extend to the England dressing-room. That is the exclusive preserve of the coach, physio and, above all, the captain and his players.

So who would I choose now the dust has settled after the World Cup? I've never been one for picking England teams even though it seems to be one of the nation's great sporting pastimes. But there are one or two key players who would always be in my side. Number one: Gough.

Next, Alec Stewart, as wicketkeeper. OK, his form with the bat hasn't been great this season and now that he has lost the captaincy there is a strong move in some quarters to shunt him aside. But I'm sure that even at 36, he has plenty of Test runs left in him and, in the absence of a truly international class all-rounder, his role of wicketkeeper-batsman enables the selectors to name five bowlers and provide a more balanced attack.

And the next two on my list would be Phil Tufnell and Andy Caddick, two of the so-called difficult players who have missed out recently because they allegedly did not fit into the concept of Team England. My firm belief has always been that if a player is good enough, he should be selected irrespective of his personality – unless, of course, he is a complete buffoon. And there is absolutely no doubt in my mind that Tufnell is head and shoulders above any other spin bowler in the English game and Caddick one of the top three pacemen.

So pick them, warts and all. Surely, the art of man management in a captain or, for that matter, coach or chairman of selectors, is the ability to handle allegedly difficult players and incorporate them into the team structure. It would be a hell of a boring world if all players were the same and any team needs its share of different personalities. Down the years, successful England sides have always contained one or two players who have been rated as 'difficult', but they have usually been winners, too. And now, more than ever, English cricket needs a successful national team.

Tufnell has been perceived as a problem boy since he first broke into the county game and then the Test set-up. In his early days he was a bit of a camel in the field and his attitude suggested that he wasn't in the business of doing anything about it. But down the years he has worked hard at his fielding to the point where he certainly doesn't have to be hidden any more. I know from experience that he isn't always the easiest-going of team-mates, though. I was on the wrong end of one of The Cat's well-publicised tantrums on the 1992–93 tour to India and Sri Lanka and I'll be talking about it later on when I look back on my own England career.

In those days, he was certainly a bit of a handful and he's had his share of problems off the field, too. But he's matured a lot and at 33, he's at his peak – a match-winner. And we haven't got so many of those around that we can afford to leave any out.

It's the same with Caddick. Ask the players on the county circuit and they will tell you that week in, week out, Caddick is as good as anyone and better than most. He proved it last season by claiming 105 Championship wickets, an incredible achievement. Yet the word is he missed out on a winter tour because he has what might be termed an individual approach to his game.

Now I've never really had anything to do with Caddick away from the middle so I cannot comment on his attitude. But I just know he's a damn good bowler and England will be cutting off their nose to spite their face if they leave him out this summer. For my money, it's certainly time to kiss and make up and give both Caddick and The Cat another chance.

HEREFORDSHIRE V YORKSHIRE, KINGTON. NATWEST TROPHY

Wednesday, 23 June. Yorkshire head south for their first game against the newest of the Minor Counties with the stigma of racism once more rearing its ugly head. Imran Khan, the former Pakistan all-rounder and captain, has used his country's appearance in the World Cup final to once again accuse Yorkshire of discriminating against players from the minority ethnic community in the county. It is a charge everyone at the club emphatically rejects. None more so than the playing staff.

We've been down this road before and no doubt it will keep on cropping up until an Asian player finally comes through the ranks and makes his Yorkshire début. When he does, we'll no doubt be accused by Imran and his like of just paying lip service to racial equality and picking a token Asian to silence the knockers.

So let me just say on behalf of all the players that as far as we are concerned, the only criterion for playing for Yorkshire is ability. If a player is good enough, it doesn't matter what his colour, race or creed is. Michael Vaughan was born in Lancashire, for heaven's sake, and we still let him in!

Imran is an educated guy thanks to The Royal Grammar School, Worcester, and Oxford University and he probably thinks we're all a bit thick up here in the northern wastelands. He may be right. But we're not so damn stupid that if there's a budding Tendulkar, Shoaib Akhtar or even a potential Imran Khan on our doorstep we're going to turn him away because of the colour of his skin. Wasn't Tendulkar, our first overseas player, an Indian? Wasn't he succeeded by Richie Richardson, a West Indian?

We have a scouting system second to none in Yorkshire and week in, week out members of our development staff are out in the schools and clubs coaching and keeping an eye out for potential Yorkshire players. Over the course of a season thousands are recommended to our cricket development officer Steve Oldham and his team. The good ones are invited to Headingley for trials. The tiny percentage who come through a rigorous assessment end up with a place in the Yorkshire Academy.

And if Imran and the rest of our critics took the trouble to take a look at the current issue of the *White Rose* magazine they would see, on page 16, a picture of this year's Academy. The first two players named in the caption are Tabassum Bhatti and Garib Razak. They are both from the Asian community and there are three more young Asian players who are currently close to a place in the Academy.

Then there's Safraz Mohammed, who is in the England Under–13 squad. Another youngster, Ridwan Patel, played in our pre-season practice games and there are 15 other kids from minority ethnic communities being coached at Yorkshire's regional Centre of Excellence. If all goes well, one or all of them will go on and establish themselves as Yorkshire first team cricketers, but they still have a long way to go. And if they are good enough no one in the world would begrudge them a place in the Yorkshire side. But no doubt if they don't make it, the old racist slur will be aired again.

On top of the young players actually involved with the club, the Yorkshire Cricket Association has set up a black and ethnic minority forum with development centres at eight venues and a summer school at Scarborough. One of our cricket development officers is Tony Bowry, a West Indian. He has a specific responsibility for black and Asian development work.

Of course it's unfortunate that in an area with such a heavy Asian population, Yorkshire have yet to unearth a player of the right calibre. But it isn't for want of trying. A couple of seasons ago, Ijaz Ahmed, the Pakistan batsman, spent a season in the Leeds League with Khalsa, an all-Asian team. Surely if he believed there was racism at the very highest level of the game in this county he would have said so. But he didn't. Instead, he went out of his way to say how keen he was to encourage Asian youngsters to play cricket in the hope of finding a youngster good enough to play for Yorkshire. Part of the problem that Ijaz found was that talented young Asians, just like English youngsters, aren't totally thrilled about turning up for net practice week in and week out. And in the past, the better players have sometimes resisted leaving their own clubs and leagues to move into the more major leagues. However, the signs are that this is starting to change.

And while we're on the subject, there's a massive Asian community in Lancashire, too. But if you take a look at Lancashire's entry in the first-class counties' playing register in the current *Playfair Annual*, you won't find any players from local minority ethnic communities. Are Lancashire ever accused of racism by Imran and Co.? Never! Like Yorkshire, of course, Lancashire would dearly love to unearth a potential Asian superstar and no doubt they will, eventually.

In the meantime, my advice to Imran is simple: If you want to see Asian players in the Yorkshire side, get yourself up to Yorkshire, talk to people at the club and then go into the Asian communities and convince talented young cricketers that there is a future for them in the first-class game with Yorkshire. In other words, adopt a positive approach instead of taking the easy option of having another pop at the Yorkshire club.

Let me repeat. The only thing we are interested in here is finding the best players for Yorkshire cricket. And as far as we are concerned it doesn't matter whether their ethnic origins are in Karachi or Cleckheaton, Hyderabad or, for that matter, Honolulu.

NatWest Trophy third round, Kington. 23 June. Yorkshire 275–8 (G. Blewett 77, A. McGrath 70) beat Herefordshire 124–5 by 151 runs.

Not a banana skin in sight. Good result, poor game. The ground at Kington was a picture and there was a smashing atmosphere but our total was just too big for them. Instead of having a go, they just blocked it out after losing a couple of early wickets. Apart from one six that forced the occupants of the Press tent to dive for cover, it was pretty boring stuff. No complaints, though; we've earned ourselves a big fourth round tie against Leicestershire at Headingley on 7 July.

YORKSHIRE V HAMPSHIRE, HEADINGLEY. BENSON & HEDGES SUPER CUP

Friday, 25 June. Yorkshire's first sortie into the new Benson & Hedges Super Cup pairs them with Hampshire, a side they have already beaten three times in one-day and four-day cricket this season.

A lot of people are saying this new Super Cup doesn't matter; that it's a meaningless competition. Those people aren't involved with the top eight sides in last season's County Championship, the teams who qualified for the Super Cup.

As far as we are concerned here in Yorkshire, we worked bloody hard over the whole of the 1998 season to finish third and qualify for this competition. And now we're involved, we want to win it. No matter that it's 99 per cent certain that next season the format will revert to early-season zonal qualifying groups before the quarter-final knockout stage.

And for me, the Super Cup has to be a strong competition because it features the eight best sides from last year's Championship. The fifty thousand pounds first prize is not to be sniffed at either. So we're up for this one, make no mistake.

From a wider viewpoint, the introduction of the Super Cup is yet another change to the way the programme is structured. It's a million miles away from the way we played the game back in 1985 and next season comes the biggest sea change of all with the start of a two-divisional County Championship. I'm 100 per cent behind the move. For the record, I'm also a big supporter of the new two-division National League with its coloured clothing, team nicknames, white balls and all the razzmatazz aimed at attracting a new audience for the game. It's an essential part of the way cricket is going in the twenty-first century.

When I made my début against Middlesex at Headingley in 1985, though, it was all three-day cricket in the Championship. The 17 counties played 24 three-day games and you don't have to be a professor of mathematics to appreciate that the figures didn't work out. We had to play eight counties twice and the others just once. A patently ludicrous situation. You could end up playing the eight best teams twice and missing out on the weaker ones.

As a youngster coming into the side I just kept quiet and got on with the business of making a name for myself. But it didn't take me long to realise that the quality of cricket being played wasn't particularly good. I'm not talking about the standard of players involved at the time because there were some great players around.

But the way the games were approached wasn't right. The team batting first would get 300 or 350, the opposition would get around 270 and then a declaration would be set up for a run chase on the third afternoon. Loads of games went down that track. You could totally outplay someone for the best part of three days but they could hang in there, get enough runs to stay in the game and then be handed a chance of winning through a declaration. As I say, ludicrous and not what the game is about.

The change to four-day cricket in 1990, at first on an experimental basis, was a blessing although initially we were messing about playing some four and some three-day games and 22 matches altogether. It was no way to run a championship. Can you imagine the FA Premiership where you play Manchester United twice, Liverpool for a game and a half and Derby County just once?

Since 1993, it's been a level playing field, at least in theory, with a four-day game against every other county, although cricket can never be totally fair because of the weather. We probably get the worst of it in the north. Last year we had two, possibly three, games when I would have put the mortgage on Yorkshire winning only to be beaten by the weather. Other counties will say it evens itself out over a season but I'm not convinced.

And then there's the pitches. Ideally, the four-day game should ensure that the team playing the best cricket over four days will win and the best players will have an opportunity to perform. Unfortunately it doesn't always work out that way because of the standard of pitches. They have definitely deteriorated during my career. When I first started the general standard was pretty reasonable but nowadays winning is so important that clubs are happy to produce a 'result' pitch, preferably in their favour. Within the regulations, of course.

So instead of games going the distance, too many are ending a day early in the interests of a result rather than the long-term benefit of English cricket. Potential Test players should be learning their trade in the best possible environment but can we honestly say that is happening in our game? Our pitches produce interesting cricket; but do they produce Test quality players?

Take a look at Australian Sheffield Shield cricket. It is played on good hard, fast tracks so if you are going to get wickets you have to bowl at express pace like Glenn McGrath or be a big spinner like Shane Warne. In this country too many mediocre dibbly-dobbly seamers can run up, put the ball there or thereabouts and pick up wickets because of the pitches. But put that kind of performer in the Test arena on a good hard surface and he travels all around the field.

We have to learn from the Aussies in this respect. OK, on the one hand we want to see results and entertaining cricket – and I'm not pretending that I don't enjoy the kind of cut and thrust cricket that we have had in so many games at Headingley over the last couple of years. But on the other hand, we have to teach bowlers to bowl people out without the help of the pitch. Until we do, we won't be able to compete with the Australians at Test match level.

So, the Blakey blueprint for the future: We need a leaner and meaner Championship structure . . . but that does not mean I advocate abandoning the county system and opting for a regional competition, far from it. There is still a lot of support at grassroots level for all the individual counties and I doubt if the prospect of the North playing the East or whatever would appeal to either players, sponsors or spectators.

But I would divide the 18 counties into two divisions of nine with just one game against each of the other counties. That's a championship of eight four-day matches played on genuine four-day pitches that give batsmen a chance to play their shots and quality pace and spin bowlers a chance to take wickets if they bowl well. Two up and two down at the end of the season.

There would be no Championship cricket until mid-May at the earliest, by which time the pitches should be less of a lottery, and absolutely no Championship games during Test matches. That would prevent counties being handicapped because they have England players.

I appreciate, of course, that there is a move to have the top players on ECB contracts in the future and that may well be in place by next season. But I would be interested to learn how it is going to work in practice. Will players like Goughie still be registered with a county? Or will they be free agents, able to pick and choose who they are going to play for? And are England going to be able to turn round and tell a player he cannot turn out in Championship games? Surely not.

If we are to have a credible County Championship as a basis for England selection, the competition has to feature current England players pitting themselves against one another eight times a season. If not, how do we measure whether a young cricketer is or isn't good enough to play Test cricket?

Competition would be intense, there would be no hiding place and no one could find a back door into the England team on the strength of good performances against weaker sides.

In an ideal world, England would select players from the top division only. In football, virtually all the international players come from Premiership sides, people who are performing against top players at the highest level week in and week out – although there must always be room for the odd maverick selection from outside the elite group.

Inevitably, that would eventually lead to a transfer system. Great! What better way to raise the profile of the game than by having big-name players moving between clubs like football.

And in answer to your question about what happens if Yorkshire end up in Division Two, I would accept that our England candidates would want to move on to further their England chances and I would expect them to do so. Me, too? Yorkshire cricket has always been my life and I have every intention of finishing my career here. But like any professional sportsman, I want to play at the highest level and would have to consider all the options.

I don't go along with the idea that a transfer system would be little more than *carte blanche* for the rich to get richer and corner the best players. It would breathe some fresh air into the game's image and represent an opportunity for the counties to get their act together on and off the field. It would also create some much-needed media coverage.

And one suggestion that has been doing the rounds for a while is that counties should trim their professional staffs. In principal, I wouldn't argue with that. Let's face it, there are too many professional cricketers. And the so-called comfort zone where contracted players are doing just enough to get a job for next year or wasting their time playing relatively meaningless Second XI cricket does exist. But why? Because there is no other option open to the county clubs. They need a professional staff of over 20 players because the game below first-class level simply isn't good enough.

We should be moving towards the Australian system where each county would have a smaller professional staff and draw on players from their local premier league. This would be at the top of the league pyramid with good pitches, good facilities and, above all, would breed players good enough to be fed into the first-class game.

This system should have been introduced years ago. But will it ever happen? I doubt it. Sadly, parochial self-interest rules OK and leagues are not prepared to abandon time-honoured traditions for the wider good of the game as a whole. In this part of the world, I certainly can't imagine the Huddersfield, Bradford, Central Yorkshire and Yorkshire leagues ever agreeing to become part of a pyramid structure and clubs would only be willing to break ranks if the prize money at stake was enormous, far more than anything that has been mentioned so far. So the county clubs are stuck with the current system of recruiting players.

Those cricketers should be playing their Championship games in midweek. Four-day cricket is still the bedrock of our game but, for better or worse, the punters don't roll up in their thousands to watch. What they are prepared to come out in large numbers for is the one-day game – so I would schedule the one-day competitions for the weekend when the vast majority of people have the time to spend a day at the cricket. That would mean the NatWest and Benson & Hedges (or whoever succeeds them as the major sponsor) knock-out matches played on a Saturday and the National League, with coloured clothing, white balls, day-night cricket and all the family attractions, on a Sunday. And as for this proposed 25-overs competition on midweek evenings . . . forget it!

Now I know someone will go away, feed all this into a computer and tell me that logistically it just wouldn't work. Typical! Let's make it work – because I believe it is the way ahead for English cricket.

Meanwhile, at Headingley, Yorkshire's superiority over Hampshire continues with a nine-wicket victory. Some hostile seam bowling, particularly from White, restricts Hampshire to 187 for 9 from their 50 overs. Yorkshire, who did not manage a single century opening stand in one-day cricket in 1998, are on cruise control this time. Byas and Blewett take them to within two of their target before the Australian is dismissed for 71, leaving Byas, with an unbeaten 104, to lead his side home with 11.2 overs to spare. In the semi-final on 10 July, Yorkshire will travel down to Edgbaston to take on Warwickshire, so often their one-day nemesis in the past.

Benson & Hedges Super Cup, Headingley. 25 June. Yorkshire 188–1 (D. Byas 104*, G.S. Blewett 71) beat Hampshire 187 by 9 wickets.

ABOVE LEFT: Young Master Blakey on his first trip to Lord's,
dreaming that one day he will play here, too

ABOVE RIGHT: Playing Huddersfield League cricket for Elland as a 16-year-old
(© *Huddersfield Examiner*)

BELOW: And some dreams come true – Blakey keeps an eye on the ball as Javed
Miandad hits out in the Texaco Trophy game against Pakistan at Lord's, 1992
(© Press Association)

1988 and an injury to David Bairstow provides one of my early opportunities to keep wicket for Yorkshire
(© *Huddersfield Examiner*)

The Phoenix rises. Byas (*left*) and McGrath join in the celebrations as I catch Darren Robinson against Essex
(© *Huddersfield Examiner*)

Wicketkeepers' Union. Sharing a joke with David Bairstow en route to a friendly winter tour of India

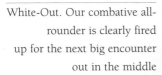

White-Out. Our combative all-rounder is clearly fired up for the next big encounter out in the middle

Exclusive . . . Goughie pictured without mobile phone and designer sunglasses

Tendulkar and I combine to seriously damage Prime Minister
John Major's hopes of re-election

Having seen off all but one of his male rivals, Lehmann prepares to turn on the style
for a captive audience

TOP LEFT: Erik The Viking. Duped into fancy dress for our 1997 Christmas party

TOP RIGHT: Hamilton, in his alternative job as a used car salesman, can't resist the temptation to celebrate another deal

BELOW: The players take time out to model next year's Yorkshire Phoenix strip

ABOVE LEFT: After missing out on England selection yet
again, Silverwood opts for a change of nationality

ABOVE RIGHT: Sorry, can't hear you. McGrath responds in
characteristic style when told: 'It's your round.'

BELOW: Using a visit to the Guinness Brewery in Dublin to bribe
Moxon (*centre*) and Vaughan into playing me as an opener

ABOVE LEFT: With my 1998 Benefit mascot Dickie Dog (*right*)

ABOVE RIGHT: Upwardly mobile. Out-of-season mode with Media Works, a marketing and PR company in Leeds

BELOW: The things we do for sponsors. Three minutes later, Gough bowled the world's first 90mph fruit pie

Yorkshire cricketers of the future? Ashton and Harrison, the next members of the Blakey dynasty

Smile please! Taking a break with Harrison and Ashton

Off duty . . . and time for a breath of fresh air with Clare

LEICESTERSHIRE V YORKSHIRE, LEICESTER

Saturday, 3 July. Yorkshire's game with County Champions Leicestershire ends more than a day early. Beaten by nine wickets, Yorkshire are bowled out for 52 before lunch on the first morning, the lowest Championship score of the season and their worst since 1973. Only once, in 1911, when they were dismissed for 49, have they performed as badly at Leicester. On a personal note, Blakey is dismissed for nought in both innings, his first pair in 14 years' first-class competition. All this after a hugely impressive performance in the National League day-night game against the same opposition when Yorkshire recorded their seventh win in eight games in the new competition.

Humiliating. There's no other word for it. And no excuses. How can there be any when a side of our so-called quality is bowled out before lunch on the first day for 52? Eight of our players have scored first-class centuries. But for ten minutes under two hours at Grace Road, we played like complete no-hopers. Nobody emerged with any credit and believe me, the dressing-room was a very quiet, very dejected place. We were shell-shocked.

Perhaps I should have known it was going to be one of those weeks when it started with the saga of the spikes. I'm normally extremely meticulous about my kit but halfway down to Leicester I realised that I hadn't ordered any new spikes for my boots. My kit supplier is Gray Nicolls and whenever I need anything I just have to give them a call and it's delivered to Headingley. This time I was too late.

Even so, I didn't reckon a few cricket spikes would cause too many problems and as the National League game was a day-night job, I strolled into town from our team hotel on Tuesday morning to buy a box of spikes. Or so I thought. Six shops later, I was reduced to buying golf spikes instead. Only a couple of weeks ago, I was saying how the World Cup had raised cricket's profile but here, in the Champion County's own territory, when I asked for cricket spikes people looked at me as if I came from the planet Zog.

Not that my footwear had any effect on our performance in the National League game for, after winning the toss, which is crucial in day-night games, we batted well, bowled even better and won by over 100 runs. Leicester are a quality side but we never let them into the game. A good performance and a good win that keeps us out in front. But as we celebrated afterwards, we never imagined in our wildest dreams what lay in store for us 36 hours down the road.

The Championship game was a very, very big match for us. Leicester are a side we have looked up to for a number of years. They have no real superstars but play well as a unit, work hard for one another and have deservedly picked up a couple of titles. We probably have a bit more quality these days but we still see them as a yardstick and in our preparations we were looking to prove we had taken the big stride forward to be up there with them.

Instead, the game was effectively over by lunch on the first day. We won the toss but even though the pitch had a bit of green in it, we were looking to weather the storm and build a decent total. OK, they bowled well and took some good catches. But there can be no disguising how badly we played. It was a pathetic display and nowhere near good enough for a side with our talent.

It was a procession. No one put together any kind of stand. Normally if a side loses five or six wickets cheaply, someone comes along and makes 50 and the score reaches a level of respectability. Not this time. I've never known anything like it in all my years in the game. It was like a snowball down a mountain.

When Greg and Virgil walked out to open the innings, I went off with Gary Fellows and Ian Fisher, the two players from the 13 who had missed out, to do some shuttle runs. I was down to bat at eight so

I figured there was time for a hard workout, a shower and a few hours with my feet up before I would be required. Wrong!

The openers survived 12 overs or so and when the first wicket went down I started to stroll back to the pavilion. Another wicket fell, I upped the pace a bit. Then there was an appeal and a round of applause meant it was three. When Mags got a first ball it was up the steps, get changed and strap on the pads time. I was still sweating from the work-out.

When I reached the dressing-room it was mayhem. There were players putting kit on or taking it off left right and centre. Before you could find your own bat, you had to duck to avoid the incoming batsman's as it flew through the air followed by a string of curses. After McGrath's dismissal, Chalkie and Dick Harden went cheaply, too, and I was on my way to the crease – for one ball.

Some day, looking back, we'll have a good laugh about it and I dread to think what the television cameras would have made of the chaotic scenes in the visitors' dressing-room. And you had to feel desperately sorry for Chris Silverwood. He woke up in his Birmingham hotel hoping to play for England against New Zealand in the first Test at Edgbaston. He learned at 10.30 a.m. that he wouldn't be required so rang Martyn Moxon to say he was on his way over to Leicester.

'There's no rush,' replied Frog. 'We've won the toss, we're batting so we won't need you for a while. No panic.' About 90 minutes later, the message was something on the lines of 'Get your ass over here, you're in next!' Silverwood arrived at the ground at 12.30, he was batting at 12.40, lasted three balls and was opening the bowling at one o'clock. No wonder he looked a bit bemused about it all.

When we went out to field ten minutes before lunch we tried to gee ourselves up. You know the kind of thing, 'Come on lads, if they can do it to us, we can bowl this lot out for 50 as well.' Realistically, though, we knew that wasn't going to happen. We took a couple of quick wickets, though, and everybody went up when we were certain Darren Maddy had nicked one down the legside to me off Silvers. Not out. He was eight at the time and as he went on to carry his bat for 185, it was a big decision. But even if he'd gone, Leicester would have probably made around 150 and that would have been enough.

Our dressing-room was very subdued at the close of play. There were a few vain attempts to raise a laugh but they went down like a lead balloon. A few of us went out for a couple of desultory beers later on but you wouldn't describe the evening as a barrel of laughs and it was a relief all round to get to bed and have an early night.

We did marginally better second time around but with a first innings deficit of around 250 there was never going to be a way back and in the end it was all we could do to avoid an innings defeat. You make your own luck and having played as poorly as we did, we got what we deserved.

It didn't help that we had a bad start in both innings. Blewie failed again, twice. And while I still don't think there is any reason to leave him out, it might be time for him to move down the order. It would make sense. After all, Darren Lehmann will be back as our overseas man next year and he will be batting at four. So we will have to find another opening batsman for the 2000 season. Why not allow Greg to fill Lehmann's position now and give someone like Matthew Wood a chance at the top of the order?

The idea of moving Blewett down has already been aired in the local press and there has even been talk of giving me the job of opener. Yes please! Like a lot of young players, I started my Yorkshire career in the Second XI going in first and when I first broke into the first team there was talk of me becoming Geoffrey Boycott's long-term successor at the top of the order. For one reason or another, mainly because of my wicketkeeping duties, that never materialised and I have gradually moved down the order to the point where I was batting number eight in the Leicester game. You don't get many chances to shine down there and I would obviously prefer to bat higher. And could I combine the roles of keeper and opener? I'd give it a damn good try.

Mind you, I'll have to perform better than I did in this game. Second time around, I collected my second leg before decision of the match, my second duck and my first pair. Wasn't I saying a few weeks ago that in 14 years I'd never bagged one? Well, they say you're not a batsman until you have, so I've earned my spurs now. I also conceded 18 byes in their first innings although, hand on heart, there wasn't a lot I could do about it. Most of the time the ball wasn't within range as it whistled past on its way to the boundary and there was another one that hit a bump in front of me and came within a whisker of taking my head with it.

Mags picked up a pair as well. And at least he had a novel excuse.

Apparently it was something to do with eating duck at lunchtime. A bad omen or something – I've heard it all now.

Needless to say, the captain had plenty to say after the game. He asked us to use our unscheduled day off to take a long, hard look at our attitude. What particularly upset him was that we had slumped from a high-quality display in the one-dayer to such an inept showing in the Championship. It hurt him a lot. It hurt me, too. He told us to look at our own individual performances and ask ourselves, deep down, if we had applied ourselves as well as we possibly could. If the answer was yes, no complaints. On balance, there will be a few negative answers.

It's Saturday night now, I'm back home and feeling very low. I've asked myself if I was properly prepared, if the attitude was right. Looking back, amid all the first-innings mayhem, I suppose it was hard for any of us to be in the right mental state.

Basically, we have to try and eradicate people coming back into the pavilion and wondering if they might have done it different. You have to go out and back yourself to get it right. And that applies in one-day and Championship games. If it doesn't work out, so be it, but don't die wondering. Quality players go out and take it on; they don't just hope to hang around for a while. And they are the players who come out on top.

After time for reflection, I accept that my contribution to the Leicester game was negligible. It's inevitable that there have been self-doubts on the journey home and right now I'm well and truly pissed off. Never mind what the sports psychologists say about positive thinking, when you have a performance like this, it isn't easy to be upbeat. I know I've been crap and there's no point deluding myself. I don't expect I'll be good company this evening.

People might try to offer consolation by reminding me that it's not the end of the world. Of course it isn't. There are a million and one things more important than the outcome of a cricket match. But don't go and tell me it's only a game. The Yorkshire players are professional sportsmen and we have performed badly. If a decorator hangs the wallpaper upside down, he doesn't go home and have a laugh about it. He worries. By the same token, if a mechanic fouls up on a service or an accountant gets his figures wrong, they will worry and brood about it. And we take our work just as seriously. Don't expect us to just shrug off this result as a bad day at the office and have a joke in the pub about it tonight. Professional sport doesn't work that way.

But having said that, tomorrow is another day. There's a big game to look forward to on Tuesday – a NatWest sixth round tie against, of all people, Leicester. The captain has told us we'll get this out of our system in the only way we really know – by hard work. We'll be in the nets at 9.30 on Monday morning and again on Tuesday and by Wednesday morning we'll be up for it again.

CGU National League, Leicester. 1 July. Yorkshire Phoenix 231–6 beat Leicestershire Foxes 131 (G.M. Hamilton 4–33) by 100 runs.
PPP Healthcare County Championship, Leicester. 7–10 July. Leicestershire 297 (D. Maddy 158) and 7–1 beat Yorkshire 52 and 251 (R.J. Harden 69, C. White 52) by 9 wickets.

YORKSHIRE V LEICESTERSHIRE, HEADINGLEY. NATWEST TROPHY

Wednesday, 7 July. Here we go again! Four days after their humiliation at Grace Road in the Championship, Yorkshire take on Leicestershire for a place in the last eight of the NatWest Trophy. Jekyll or Hyde? To wholesale relief on White Rose territory, Yorkshire show the better side of their nature and win, with something to spare.

The attitude has been excellent since the Leicester débâcle. Two hard days in the nets and everyone worked their bollocks off. In itself, of course, that was no guarantee that we would perform any better in a very important NatWest tie against the same quality opposition. But this time, it just felt right. It wasn't a faultless performance because there's still some work to do with the bowling and when we lost our first three wickets for 14 the target of 230 looked formidable, to put it mildly.

I've played in many Yorkshire sides who would have rolled over and slumped to 120 all out. But I never felt for a minute that we would lose this one. Mags and Michael Vaughan played out of their skin. No praise can be too high for them because they kept up with the rate right from the moment they came together. High quality stuff, Yorkshire cricket at its best and everyone on the balcony was willing them to see it through.

But first Virgil got out, then Dick Harden didn't hang around and it was left to Mags and Gavin Hamilton to stabilise the ship a bit. They looked to have got it together again when Gav tweaked a hamstring and the fun started. As Vaughan had spent most of the innings at the crease, he volunteered to act as a runner. A very brave man with Gavin around.

Inevitably it wasn't many minutes before Gavin called Mags for a single, set off himself, went back and all three ended up at the same end. Pure Keystone Cops, particularly when all three realised their mistake and turned round for their home port once more. The outcome was three overthrows and even the Leicester players had to smile.

The only person who didn't see the funny side at the time was one R.J. Blakey who was padded up, waiting to go in next. Now I've said before that batting with Gavin can be a mercurial experience even when there isn't a third party involved in the shape of a runner. And when Mags was out with just a handful of runs needed, I set off down the pavilion steps with some trepidation.

I was reassured to see a reception committee waiting for me in the shape of Hamilton and Vaughan, a sensible, clear-thinking guy in all situations. Or almost all. They had worked out ahead of my arrival that Gavin would do all the calling, irrespective of whether the ball travelled behind or in front of the wicket. Fair enough, in theory.

In practice, I was just getting the feel of things when Gavin played a ball backward of point and, as I prepared to embark on what can safely be described as one of the most straightforward singles in one-day cricket history, shouted 'No!'

I was more or less committed even at that early stage in proceedings and knew I didn't have to be Linford Christie to get home with plenty to spare. 'Bollocks, I'm coming,' was the Blakey reply in a nutshell. Vaughan, 35 yards away at square leg, didn't seem to hear either call and was sauntering around in a little world of his own.

At one stage, it looked as if all three Yorkshire batsmen would be stranded at the same end again but Michael got his act together and, with the aid of another overthrow, reached safety.

With four needed to win I decided it was time to get it over with, stroked the winning boundary and we all retired to the hutch with another tale to tell the grandchildren. And another one-day win for Yorkshire.

As I say, I never had any doubts. I spent quite a long time sitting on the balcony waiting padded up but it was one of those days when I felt completely at ease about the whole thing. I knew deep down in my bones that I would go out there and win the match for my side, even with the prospect of Hamilton and a runner on the immediate horizon.

Why? I honestly can't tell you. Waiting to bat is a funny business and no two players and no two days are the same. Some players prefer to sit quietly on their own; others like to have a chat and a laugh to take their minds off it. Personally I like the quiet approach but even then, I can sometimes be calm and confident and at other times edgy and twitchy. There are days when I hardly even notice there are other players around and days when they constantly get on my nerves.

After facing just four balls in two innings against Leicester in the Championship disaster at Grace Road and making one not out from a single delivery in the day-night game, I should logically have been all wound up for this one. Instead, I knew when I walked out that I was giving off the right vibes and I was already working out where I would score my first run.

People always say cricket is played in the mind and I would never argue with that. And nowhere do the mind games come into it more than when you have to sit on the balcony for a couple of hours awaiting your turn to bat.

NatWest Trophy fourth round, Headingley. 7 July. Yorkshire 233–6 (M.P. Vaughan 85, A. McGrath 84) beat Leicestershire 229–9 by 4 wickets.

WARWICKSHIRE V YORKSHIRE, EDGBASTON. BENSON & HEDGES SUPER CUP SEMI-FINAL

Saturday, 10 July. Yorkshire's NatWest victory over Leicestershire has earned them a quarter-final tie with Lancashire and a chance to settle old scores at Old Trafford on 28 July. In the meantime, there is unfinished business to attend to in the shape of a Super Cup semi-final against Warwickshire at Edgbaston followed by games against the same opposition in the Championship and National League.

I've had mixed feelings about Edgbaston since 1995 when it was the scene of my most embarrassing moment on a cricket field. It's amazing that four years on, people still come up and remind me about The Day Blakey Puked. There will be a few at Edgbaston this weekend, mark my words.

It was a Sunday League game. The Yorkshire players had been staying overnight at a hotel down the Hagley Road, just a few minutes from the ground, and some of us had eaten in the hotel restaurant. It was an important game so after the meal, we just had a couple of quiet beers and then an early night.

I felt a bit queasy when I first woke up and breakfast didn't exactly appeal. But I thought nothing of it and it wasn't until I set off for the ground that I started to feel really awful. Violent stomach pains, and clear signs that I was going to be sick in the not too distant future, more or less convinced me that I wouldn't be fit to play. Therefore I decided to have a word with the skipper when we arrived at the pavilion.

Unfortunately, by the time I made it into the dressing-room, Craig White was already locked in the toilet being sick and was clearly in no fit state to turn out. As we only had 12 players, I decided to keep quiet and hope for the best.

Instead, it was the worst. Warwickshire won the toss, we were required to field first and as you might expect, life for a wicketkeeper is even more frantic in the Sunday League than in Championship cricket. The constant squatting and up and down motion is one thing but running up to the stumps virtually every ball makes life even more difficult. It soon became obvious that it was only a matter of time before I joined Chalkie in the throwing-up stakes.

In the end, it was a race against time as I waited for a long throw to come in from the boundary. As soon as the ball landed in my gloves, I hurled the ball to the nearest fielder, sprinted away from the wicket and threw up. Needless to say, sympathy from team-mates, the Warwickshire batsmen and even the umpires was not forthcoming. Everybody seemed to think it was a huge joke. So, too, did a fair number of the assembled throng who spotted what was happening and started to chant 'Hughie! Hughie!' in my direction, a gesture which alerted the rest of the punters to my plight.

The groundsman was called upon to perform the mopping-up operations with the help of a bag of sawdust and a notable lack of enthusiasm for the task in hand. And after a few desultory enquiries about the state of my health from my White Rose colleagues, play got under way again.

For a brief spell, I felt a bit better and thought I might get away with it. But after another five overs or so, the familiar rumblings started down below and I was violently sick once again. This time, two distinctly disgruntled groundsmen came on, armed with a shovel and a sweeping brush. And instead of a handful of fans chanting at my expense, virtually the whole crowd joined in.

I tried to give it another try but clearly enough was enough. And three overs later, to the amusement of 21 players, two umpires and about 3,000 fans, I made my way gingerly towards the sanctuary of the pavilion. Chalkie had started to perk up a bit but he was clearly less than thrilled to be taking my place.

Warwickshire mustered 175 for 6 from their 38 overs, and when it was our turn to bat I was flat out on a dressing-room bench. There were one or two dark mutterings in the camp about Blakey not fancying his chances against Allan Donald on a corrugated iron track but the lads could see I was in a pretty horrendous state. If it had been nip and tuck at the end of the match I would have gone out to face the music. But thankfully, I was excused batting duties. Well, we were 56 for 9!

I subsequently learned that a couple of journalists who were at the same hotel had also been taken ill and were later diagnosed as suffering from a severe bout of food poisoning. So it goes without saying that I urged the Yorkshire hierarchy to find alternative accommodation on future visits to Edgbaston. Thankfully they took the idea on board and we're about to set off for our Super Cup semi-final with a clean bill of health.

This time there are no gremlins on or off the field and Yorkshire beat Warwickshire by 56 runs to reach their first Lord's final since 1987. Their Man of the Match is Craig White, once regarded as the answer to England's search for an all-rounder, who hits 55 at a run a ball before claiming 1 for 17 from eight overs as Warwickshire attempt to cut loose in pursuit of Yorkshire's 50-over total of 219 for 8. Blakey is the only survivor from the side that won the Benson & Hedges Trophy in the last final 12 years ago.

Delight, pure delight. For my team-mates, the supporters and everyone connected with Yorkshire cricket. And for me, too. After all, this has been a long time coming. If you'd told me when we won the Benson & Hedges all those years ago that Yorkshire would not be in another Lord's final until 1999, I would have suggested a trip to the nearest psychiatrist. Particularly if you'd also said I would be the only survivor from that side and I would be batting at eight and keeping wicket in our semi-final victory. Yes, times have changed!

But this makes all the near misses worthwhile. We've played in five semi-finals in the last five years and lost them all. We've been labelled chokers. And needless to say the merchants of doom were predicting another defeat this time around. But I knew when I woke up this morning that the vibes were good. Everything felt right; our time had come. And if we can go to Lord's and win, I am convinced it will be the breakthrough we are craving. Victory can be the start of something really big for Yorkshire cricket.

It wasn't plain sailing, of course. We went into the match without Gough, Hamilton and Hutchison, three international-class bowlers, and Hoggard was by no means 100 per cent after missing a couple of weeks with a knee problem. Yes, I know, Warwickshire were without Allan Donald, a man who has given us more than our fair share of grief down the years, but on balance our loss was greater than theirs.

After Chalkie had given us a flier with his 55 from as many balls, we slipped a bit in the middle order. At 121 for 5, it could have gone either way. But once again, we dug deep and clawed our way back, as we have done so often in one-day cricket this season. And while a 50-over total of 219 for 8 was perhaps a bit under par, it was always going to be useful. Things were looking a bit iffy when they were 80-odd for 1 after 18 overs but Craig and Michael Vaughan applied the brake when it was needed and we were home with 9.1 overs to spare. Inevitably, Chalkie landed the Gold Award.

So what a difference a week makes! Last Saturday, it was Greta Garbo time, I just wanted to be alone after that disaster at Leicester. Now let's party. Some of the lads are staying down in Birmingham because we start a Championship match against Warwickshire on Tuesday. But I'm heading back up the road for a night out with some friends in Harrogate. Festivities commence at 10.30 p.m. and it will be a long, hard night. So put the bubbly on ice . . . I'm on my way!

Benson & Hedges Super Cup, semi-final. Yorkshire 219–8 (C. White 55) beat Warwickshire 163 by 58 runs.

WARWICKSHIRE V YORKSHIRE, EDGBASTON

Tuesday, 13 July. Hangovers repaired, Yorkshire's one-day heroes return to Edgbaston for their tenth Championship engagement of the season. After successive defeats by Sussex and Leicestershire, they know that a third failure here will almost certainly end their title hopes. Now in ninth place, they are also hovering on the cut-off zone for next year's two-division competition. A far cry from those heady predictions of Championship glory back in April. Neither side is certain whether their fast bowling champion will be in action. Yorkshire's Darren Gough will test his injured calf in the nets on match day while Warwickshire's Allan Donald is struggling with the ankle problem that ruled him out of the Super Cup match.

Donald is probably the best fast bowler I have ever faced, and certainly one of the fastest. I have a tremendous amount of admiration for him. My views on fast bowling are well-known . . . it's bloody hard work; one of the toughest jobs in sport. And while coming back for a third spell at the end of a long day in front of a full house in a Lord's Test is enough to get the adrenaline flowing, it's a totally different ball game in front of three men and a dog on a wintry evening at Guildford or Maidstone. Not for Donald it isn't.

I have never known him throttle back and not give 100 per cent. Those steely eyes will still be staring you down whether the scoreboard reads 50 for 5 or 250 for 1. Down the years he's been a tremendous

player for Warwickshire and must surely be rated one of the top
overseas players of all time.

When Yorkshire first entered the overseas market there was a lot of
excitement about signing Australia's Craig McDermott, widely
regarded as the world's leading fast bowler at that time. It didn't work
out because of injury, we signed Sachin Tendulkar instead and we've
stuck with batsmen ever since. Elsewhere, though, the theory persists
in some quarters that all a county has to do is whistle up an overseas
fast bowler, let him loose on English batsmen and wait for the trophies
to roll in. It doesn't work out that way.

The overseas fast bowlers who have really done the business since I
was capped by Yorkshire in 1987, include men like Malcolm Marshall,
Courtney Walsh, Wasim Akram and Donald.

But far too many of them have come into county cricket without
realising what a bloody tough job they have taken on. Every now and
then, particularly on a big occasion, they will run in as if it's a Test
match and turn on the kind of match-winning performance they are
paid a lot of money to provide. But at other times they will feel a bit
of a twinge or they will be stiff after a hard day and they will only jog
in and go through the motions. That's not what their county is
looking for and not what English cricket wants from the overseas
men.

But not Donald. The Warwickshire players and members cannot
speak highly enough of his attitude. And I recall hearing that when he
had a season as Rishton's professional in the Lancashire League, he was
first on the ground in the morning to mark up the wicket and one of
the last to leave after buying the members a drink. Needless to say, they
won the championship that year and Donald took 106 wickets at
10.75. Less predictably, he scored 389 runs, too.

I used to think he saved up his most menacing performances
specially for Yorkshire but talk to any of the lads on the circuit and
they will recount similar tales of woe. At times, he has been almost
unplayable against us and there was certainly a period when he
exercised a psychological stranglehold on the team.

That did not apply, however, in our Benson & Hedges quarter-final
at Headingley in 1991. When I joined David Byas at the fall of the third
wicket, we needed to start pushing things along. Now neither of us can
quite remember whose idea it was . . . but we evolved a plot that we

could sneak a few quick singles and cause a spot of mayhem by running when the ball went through to the wicketkeeper, Keith Piper.

With Donald operating at high pace, he was standing about 30 yards back so we reckoned that with a full sail and a following wind we would make it more often than not. So the next time Bingo played and missed, I got my head down and went for it. You can imagine that it caused a certain amount of surprise and consternation among the Warwickshire lads, particularly Piper. A couple of balls later, it was my turn to play and miss and off we went again.

In two Donald overs we notched up four or five and while we were discussing the next moves between overs, Warwickshire's captain Andy Lloyd approached us. He was not best pleased. 'Look lads, I admire your tactics but you're backing up too far and if you carry on, we'll will run you out without a warning.' We just nodded and said fair enough . . . and next ball, we ran again.

The response was to post a slip and when Piper caught the ball, he threw it to the slip who, according to the plan, would shy at the stumps and leave the Yorkie batsman stranded yards out of his crease. All worked according to plan – until the throw missed the stumps and we ran overthrows.

It started to reach farcical proportions when they then put a short leg in, telling the wicketkeeper to throw the ball to slip . . . slip to move it on to short leg . . . short leg to remove the bails with, once again, the Yorkie stranded. That didn't work either. Even Donald, normally a composed customer, was starting to lose his cool and he loosed off a couple of wides at one stage. It couldn't last, of course. And it didn't. But it sure was fun while it lasted and we went on to win the match by 111 runs. And, believe it or not, our match-winner was Martyn Moxon, with figures of 5 for 31.

Two years later, Donald exacted terrible revenge in a NatWest quarter-final at Headingley. His presence has never loomed larger. This time I joined David when we were 69 for 5, chasing 246. *Wisden* described our innings up to that point as '29 overs of strokeless indecision, especially against Donald.' And even though I ended up with 75 and shared a sixth wicket stand of 105 with Chalkie, we subsided 21 runs short.

By all accounts, Donald is doubtful for the Championship game this week. And while he doesn't strike terror into the hearts of the current generation of Yorkshire batsmen, we won't be crying in our beer if he misses out.

In fact, Donald did miss out and Yorkshire cashed in with the victory that keeps alive their Championship hopes. It was a close-run thing, though, and at 106 for 5 in pursuit of their target of 223, defeat loomed. Gavin Hamilton, with an undefeated 75, Richard Harden and, at the death, Blakey saw them home. Batting at nine, his lowest position in 14 years of first-class cricket, Blakey scored 17 from 24 balls to seal victory.

We were looking down both barrels at one stage but Hamilton played tremendously well. Harden, too. And afterwards, Gavin paid glowing tributes to his partners. He said how well Dick had played and then described yours truly as 'surely the best number nine in the game.' Well, Gav, thanks for the compliment, but you just happened to touch a bit of a raw nerve with that one.

I've never been a man to blow my own trumpet but if I'm not one of the best number nines around then there's something wrong. At the start of the season, I had 11,812 first-class runs to my name at an average of 32.01 with ten centuries and 70 half-centuries. I've passed 1,000 runs in a season five times and toured with England A twice as a specialist batsman. In 1987, after scoring 1,361 first-class runs at an average of 41.24 and with a top score of 204 not out, I was voted Young Cricketer of the Year by the Cricket Writers. Not bad for a number nine, you might say.

So what am I doing messing about so low in the order? Well, let's look at the players above me. In this game, for instance, we fielded six specialist batsmen in Vaughan, Wood, Byas, Blewett, McGrath and Harden. White, who averaged almost 40 last season and has batted at number six for England, was at seven and Hamilton at eight. Gavin made runs against some of the best bowlers in the game in the World Cup, he's been in good nick and I can understand them wanting to push him forward because he is the future of Yorkshire cricket. One day he'll almost certainly be batting at five or six. I edged in at nine ahead of Goughie, although Darren has a first-class century to his name and no doubt feels he's worth better than number ten.

I've spent most of the last two seasons at seven but this time I've slipped down the order to eight and now nine, even though I have been playing reasonably well. David had a word with me before the game and told me that with so many good players around, I would have to go in at nine. I'm sure he knew how disappointed I was but it's a captain's job to take decisions in the interests of the team.

So I understand where he is coming from and like David, I've always put the team first, last and everything. But that doesn't stop me being more than a little bit pissed off about batting so low, because I honestly believe it doesn't enable me to make the contribution I want to the team effort.

Let's take the one-day game. I've been around a long time and played a lot of one-day innings high up the order. And in all fairness, I've played some good knocks down the years. I certainly feel that I have something to offer in terms of experience and know-how in the middle order; an ability to work the ball around and assess the situation as it develops. Batting at eight or nine can be important, of course and already this season, I've guided us home on a few occasions. But there's no opportunity to seriously influence the course of events and with my experience I feel I am in a position to do exactly that.

And while I haven't got the quantity of runs I would have liked in Championship cricket, I have played some important innings for the team. Like my 17 not out in this last game. It was still very much touch and go when I went in but Gavin and I put on 37 to finish the job nicely. It might have been a very different story if I had gone quickly. I played positively and well. But at the end of the season, 17 not out won't be registered in the hall of fame.

Down the years I have drifted from batsman to batsman-wicketkeeper to wicketkeeper-batsman. It's frustrating. And without denigrating players who traditionally bat down at nine, ten and jack, I know I'm worth better.

PPP Healthcare County Championship, Edgbaston. Yorkshire 213 (A. McGrath 75) & 224–7 (G.M. Hamilton 75*) beat Warwickshire 253 (N.V. Knight 59, D. Gough 4–62) & 182 (D. Gough 3–45, C. White 3–26) by 3 wickets.

WARWICKSHIRE BEARS V YORKSHIRE PHOENIX, EDGBASTON & GLOUCESTERSHIRE GLADIATORS V YORKSHIRE PHOENIX, CHELTENHAM. CGU NATIONAL LEAGUE

Saturday, 17 July. Donald returns to the Warwickshire side for the National League and once again Yorkshire show the worse side of their Jekyll and Hyde nature. They fare no better at Cheltenham 24 hours later, suffering another defeat that plunges their one-day title hopes into disarray. The long journey home is a grim affair.

It's been a nightmare. Two National League games, two defeats. Two wins and we would have had one hand on the trophy. As it is, our lead has slipped away and if Worcestershire win tomorrow they will take over at the top. Lancashire are closing up in third place. The only consolation is that we still have to play Worcester at Headingley and two day-night games against the Lankies. So we're still very much in contention. But we could easily have been over the horizon, leaving the rest to sort out the runners-up spot.

Yet again, we've let ourselves down with a couple of shoddy performances. We posted 213 against Warwickshire and on one of our better days that would have been enough. But we bowled and fielded poorly. And we got everything wrong at Cheltenham, in the process giving Gloucester, our Super Cup final opponents, a big psychological lift for Lord's.

Silvers and I hardly exchanged a word as we drove home from

Cheltenham apart from polite enquiries about which tape to put on next. And the general sense of gloom isn't helped by the fact that we're in the middle of a long spell on the road. I snatched a couple of days at home after the Super Cup semi-final last weekend but some of the boys stayed down in Birmingham and were away from their families for ten nights. A long time.

The last stopover was in Cheltenham on Saturday. We jumped into our cars straight after the Warwickshire game and drove in convoy down the M5, stopping off at a motorway service station for a bite to eat. Quite a few of the lads had stiffened up by the time we reached the hotel in Cheltenham, which was hot and noisy. None of us got much sleep and it's on days like this that you wake up feeling as if you've been hit by a bus. I'm not using that as an excuse for a performance that simply wasn't up to the professional standards we set ourselves . . . but it didn't help.

Now, after just one night at home, we're off to Scarborough for a four-day game against Northants and a National League match with Kent which will mean being away for another six nights.

I got home at around midnight, completely pissed off. I couldn't even be bothered unpacking the car and just mumbled a few words to Clare before staggering off to bed. This morning it's been a case of get up, put the washer on, fire three loads of kit into the tub, mow the lawn, dry the washing and pack up again. Then I'll hit the road to Scarborough mid-afternoon. It's a tough schedule and it's certainly designed to test personal relationships and marriages.

Now don't get me wrong. I feel privileged to have spent 16 years playing cricket for Yorkshire. It's been a wonderful experience and I wouldn't have changed it for the world. I also have two England A tours and a full England tour to add to my CV. And a broken marriage two years ago.

It's hard enough being away for such long spells when things are going well but it's even tougher when there are problems at home. Your mind is split in two. One half knows that being away is part and parcel of the job; the other half wants to be back home sorting things out. Cricket affects your home life. Domestic problems inevitably affect your cricket but the job still has to be done.

I've no doubt that a lot of people out there look at the life of a county cricketer and think glamour. What could be better than being paid to play sport? Hotels, nights out with the boys, wine, women and song. Most of that went out with the ark. The groupies have discovered football and while cricket still has a healthy social life, the days of Test players reporting for duty on the morning of the match in last night's dinner jacket are long gone. Most of the hotels we use are modern, clean and comfortable but they aren't home and living out of a suitcase is a tough existence. I can't think of many cricketers who wouldn't swap life in a hotel room for their own home, their own kitchen, their own sofa, their own bed, their own bathroom.

Hotels can be lonely places and it's no fun being stuck in a twin-bedded room at the other end of the country when one of the kids is poorly or the boiler has just blown up and you're helpless to do anything about it.

I have two little boys, Harrison who will be six in September, and Ashton who's four. They live with their mum but I take every opportunity I can to spend time with them. They're just starting to get into cricket and I love every minute I spend with them. But when we have long spells on the road like this, it inevitably means they aren't going to see their dad for a while and I really miss them. It's the price I have to pay for being a professional sportsman.

It's a great life and it's given me friendships and memories I will cherish for the rest of my days. But I just wanted the people out there to know there's a down side, too.

Enough of the soul-searching. Life can be funny even when you're losing and we all had a good laugh at Dick Harden's expense down in Cheltenham. Poor old Dick was struggling with a bad back and a dodgy knee when he hauled himself out of bed and just about made it as far as the bathroom for an invigorating shower. Unfortunately when he turned on the water supply, the shower head, made of solid stainless steel, flew off the piping and gave him a fearful clatter on the skull. Next time he stays in Cheltenham, the helmet goes into the shower with him.

CGU National League, Edgbaston. 17 July. Yorkshire 213 (M.P. Vaughan 72, A. McGrath 71) lost to Warwickshire 214–5 by 5 wickets.

CGU National League, Cheltenham. 18 July. Yorkshire 133 (M. Ball 5–42) lost to Gloucestershire 261 (R.C. Russell 91*) by 128 runs.

YORKSHIRE V NORTHAMPTONSHIRE, SCARBOROUGH

Friday, 23 July. Yorkshire's Championship hopes take a nose-dive when they fail to beat Northants, the bottom club. The good news for Greg Blewett is a total of 288 runs, his long-awaited first century for the county and a match-saving performance. The bad news for Blakey is a dislocated finger . . . ten days away from Yorkshire's first Lord's final in 12 years.

Anthony McGrath was bowling and we were well into the second afternoon with Northants steaming on past 400 after being put into bat and losing their first three wickets for 17. Not a happy day for the White Rose, and certainly not for me. It was an innocuous delivery that kept a bit low. The batsman played and missed, the ball hit me on the end of the middle finger of my left hand and I knew immediately that something was very wrong.

You try not to make a fuss. I whipped my glove off to discover that the finger was pointing in the wrong direction. Dislocated. There was no pain at first, although just looking at the finger made me feel a bit queasy, not least because we've a NatWest quarter-final coming against Lancashire on Wednesday and the Super Cup final at Lord's next Sunday. And I don't intend to miss out on those two.

The pain started to kick in as the ligaments around the joint worked out that there was something amiss and responded angrily. Sometimes with these injuries, you can push the finger back into place and carry on as if nothing has happened. But our physio Caryl Becker tried without success and it was the same story when the Northants physio had a go.

So it was get in the car time and off to Scarborough hospital. I had a couple of X-rays to establish there was no break and then two painkilling injections before the doctor could make the necessary repairs. He said it was a nasty one and as I made my way back to the ground the finger was very swollen.

I've had ultrasound treatment as well as icepacks and the swelling has gradually gone down. Three days on, the finger looks more or less normal but it is very, very tender. I've gone through seven shades of agony every time I've taken a ball and batting is a painful business, to put it mildly.

So where do I go from here? With two massive games coming up, this is all I need. But if it's just a question of putting up with the pain, obviously I'll give it a go. If there was a break and I had been ruled out for a month it would have felt like the end of the world. But it isn't. It's dislocated, it hurts like hell but I'm a Yorkshire cricketer and I want to be out there helping the lads reach the last four of the NatWest and win the Super Cup.

I've never been one for heroics so I'll keep quiet about it. After netting before the final day against Northants, Martyn Moxon asked me how it felt. I just smiled and said it was fine. And made tracks before he could ask any seriously awkward questions. Having said that, though, he's had enough finger injuries himself to know it isn't really all right at all; but he also knows all about playing through the pain barrier.

It wasn't all bad news, though. My injury gave first White and, as I didn't keep wicket in the Northants second innings, McGrath a chance to take over the gloves. Chalkie is a jack of all trades and he's done it before. In fact, when he was at the Australian Academy he was regarded as a keeper of real potential. But I think it was a first-timer for Mags and, needless to say, he took a blinding catch. It will be a while before I hear the last of it.

And Greg Blewett finally came good, although he just could not believe it when he was out leg before for 98 in the first innings – not offering a shot. For an eternity, he sat gazing into the middle distance. Probably no one can really appreciate his relief when he finally reached three figures after we had followed on. He's never been through anything like this in the whole of his career. Even though his record says he's world-class, he's put together one low score after another – and he has the added responsibility of carrying high expectations as the overseas man. But this surface was a bit more like the ones he's used to back home and he took his chance.

It will always be to his credit that he has kept his innermost feelings from the rest of the players. He's a strong character, he's kept working for the team and on his own game and above all, he's kept smiling. You cannot fault his attitude, but at the end of the day he's here to do a job and he hasn't been doing it. And whoever you are, however tough you may be, the tension shows through in the end.

We have a day off before the National League game against Kent on Sunday, so Friday night is party night. A much needed blow-out after a long stretch on the road. And no one deserves a drink more than Blewie. He leaves us early in August to link up with the Australians for their tour of Sri Lanka and I just hope he can go out with a bang. I'd like to remember him as the man who helped Yorkshire back on to the trophy trail.

It has become a Yorkshire tradition for county caps to be awarded at Scarborough. Last year, Gavin Hamilton and Paul Hutchison were the recipients. This time Anthony McGrath, who made his début in 1995 and has twice toured with England A, gains his reward for a consistent season in both Championship and one-day cricket.

I've a lot of time for McGrath and I'm delighted to see him capped. It's richly deserved. He's been our best batsman this season. I mentioned right at the start of the book that his nose was put out of joint by the signing of Dick Harden from Somerset during the winter. After an indifferent time last year, McGrath's place was clearly on the line. But once his request to be released had been predictably turned down, he dug in and vowed to secure a regular place.

He's a good player and at 23, there is every scope for him to go on to become a very good one indeed. He's a big lad and needs to keep an eye on his fitness but he worked hard in Australia over the winter and now he's reaping the reward. If he plays straight, 'in the V' as we say, there aren't many better strikers of the ball. When he first came into the game people predicted a very big future for him but the last couple of years have been tough. But for me, the application and attitude he has shown this season suggest that he can go on and fulfil that potential. Being capped should help.

Until recently, caps were awarded in a little ceremony in front of the pavilion before the start of play. That's what happened when I was capped in 1987. But somehow, with the spectators still coming into the ground or finding their seats, the occasion tended to be overlooked. And that's a shame. Being capped is a big day in a player's career.

So when David took over as captain he revived a very old tradition of the skipper handing the player his cap out in the middle during the game. This time, the skipper had a word with the umpires on the first day and they took Mags's cap and first team sweater out on to the pitch. Then Byas called the Yorkshire players together and handed Mags his cap and sweater in front of over 2,000 supporters. It's a nice touch and something we should preserve.

Mags, or Gripper as we sometimes call him, is a likeable lad. His only major personality defect is that he's a fanatical Manchester United supporter. As a matter of interest, he's also a helluva good footballer, easily the best on the Yorkshire staff – despite what Hamilton might say! He's also the leading prankster and the early front-runner when we were trying to identify the Phantom Sock Snipper. I would have backed him then, although now I'm not so sure. The Phantom has been dormant all season and Mags could never adopt such a low profile.

Mind you, he's been on the receiving end plenty of times as well, never more so than in the Sheffield Fish War. It must have been two years ago. Mags and Alex Morris, who moved to Hampshire with Peter Hartley last year, had been playing tricks on one another all season and, as tends to happen in these sagas, things started to get a bit nasty.

I've mentioned before that the dressing-room at Sheffield is a bit cramped and tempers tend to get frayed when we're changing, particularly at the end of a hard day in the field. And Morris, who had already had the peak of his cap removed earlier in the season, was decidedly unimpressed when he put his small change into his trouser pocket only to see it rolling around the dressing-room floor a few seconds later – to the evident delight of McGrath.

So when Morris retreated to his Barnsley home to consider his next course of action, muttering 'I'm going to do him once and for all,' we sensed things were moving towards an ominous conclusion for McGrath. The following morning, Almo arrived at the ground with an air of self-satisfaction and a parcel under his arm which, when opened, revealed a fresh mackerel – full length: head, tail, the lot. And with Mags safely embarked on his warm-up, the offending fish was stuffed down one of his pads between the outer case and the bolster that offers added protection. The lads were agog to see if McGrath would spot anything fishy, if you'll pardon the pun.

But when his time came to bat, he strapped on his left pad, then his right, clearly oblivious to the atmosphere of suppressed hilarity among his team-mates. In due course, he ambled out to the middle and needless to say, during the course of his innings pad and fish were struck several times. When he returned to the pavilion, the pads were unstrapped and hurled into his kit coffin along with the rest of his batting equipment. Clothing followed at the close of play.

The third day was wiped out by rain so when we returned to resume hostilities on the final day, we were greeted by a horrendous stench emanating from the home dressing-room. Everyone was going around sniffing in corners, pretending they had no idea where it was coming from and waiting for the magical moment when Gripper would open his coffin. When he did, the smell was truly appalling. By this time, the mackerel was well down on its luck and the stink had infected his pads, gloves and all the rest of his gear. The only option was for Mags to chuck the whole lot over the balcony never to be seen again. Definitely one to Morris that time.

It's appropriate that Gripper should be capped at Scarborough as well, because back in his first season he almost didn't make it to North Marine Road after being called up as a late replacement. He wasn't too sure of the route but was told to take M62, A1 North, A64. Can't go wrong. Mags did OK until he hit the A1 but then instead of playing the numbers game and taking the A64, he looked for signs to Scarborough. There aren't any. It just says A64 York.

The distress call was answered in the dressing-room by Goughie and went something on the lines of, 'I'm struggling a bit. I've made it to Scotch Corner and there still aren't any signs for Scarborough.' He finally arrived just before the start of play and had to take a load of stick about his knowledge of local geography. I suppose the pranks we have had to put up with ever since are probably his way of taking revenge.

Having said that, though, only the intervention of a vigilant lifeguard guaranteed Mags's involvement in our season, never mind winning a county cap. It happened in Durban on our pre-season tour. After a particularly rigorous day on the training ground and in the nets, Mags and I decided to head for the beach in the early evening. Mags opted for a swim; I flopped down on a sunbed to take in the sights, which in that particular neck of the woods are very shapely.

I tried to keep an eye out for Mags as he frolicked in the foaming brine, patiently returning his frequent waves. But waving to a blond Englishman did little for my macho image and eventually I found myself dozing off. I was rudely awakened some 20 minutes later by an angry McGrath, demanding why I hadn't responded to his SOS calls. It turned out that the waving was a frantic effort to tell me he was in trouble. Thankfully, the lifeguard spotted him, launched the rescue boat and an embarrassed Mags was hauled aboard and rowed to safety. He was not amused.

Still, good luck to you, Mags, congratulations on the cap and thanks for the celebratory glass of champagne.

PPP Healthcare County Championship, Scarborough. 20–23 July. Yorkshire 289 (G.S. Blewett 98) & 407 (Blewett 190, G.M. Hamilton 84*) drew with Northants 517–7 dec. (A.L. Penberthy 123, D. Ripley 107*, D.J.G. Sales 101) & 61–2.

YORKSHIRE PHOENIX V KENT SPITFIRES, SCARBOROUGH. NATIONAL LEAGUE

Sunday, 25 July. Things go from bad to worse. After an inept Championship showing against Northants, Yorkshire slither to their third successive National League defeat in front of a packed Scarborough house. There are distinct mutterings of discontent among the members.

Why have we gone off the boil? I honestly don't know. But since we beat Warwickshire in the Super Cup semi-final our cricket has, to put it mildly, been poor. We've collected three defeats on the bounce in the National League, we were under par in the Championship win over Warwickshire and distinctly second best for three of the four days against Northants. We only scraped out of that one because of some marvellous batting by Greg and another good innings from Gavin.

I hesitate to blame the Super Cup. When we qualified for the Lord's final I strongly believed it would enable us to move up a couple of notches in our National League and Championship form. Instead we've gone the other way and lost a lot of ground in both competitions. I can say for a fact that none of the players has lifted his foot off the gas since reaching Lord's, not least because places in the final are at stake. But maybe it's a sub-conscious thing. All I know is that we're not firing at the moment, the intensity isn't there. OK, tiredness is creeping in. But if you are a successful side playing high-velocity games, that's something you have to overcome. And unless we find another gear we'll be struggling in the NatWest quarter-final at Old Trafford on Wednesday.

Injuries don't help, of course, and the fast bowling line-up I was so confident about has taken a real pounding from day one. Goughie is struggling with the calf injury that has kept him out of the first two Tests and there's no way he'll be back for Old Trafford or Lord's. Paul Hutchison has been out all season with his back problem and played his first game against Kent today after re-modelling his action to avoid a repetition and Matthew Hoggard has had minor surgery on a knee injury and may need another operation in the winter. On top of those three, Gavin was unable to bowl today because of a sore back, Chalkie is struggling with a hip injury, Silvers has had a dodgy knee and Ryan Sidebottom is suffering from wear and tear and needs a rest. It's anyone's guess as to who will be fit from one game to the next. But we'll battle on.

Injuries are just part and parcel of a cricketer's life and I can honestly say that the days in a season when I can stand up and claim to be absolutely 100 per cent fit can just about be counted on one hand. Last season's knee and groin niggles and an aching back more or less sorted themselves out over the winter only to return as soon as we started playing in earnest.

Earlier in my career I used to suffer from horrendous migraine attacks that would hit me like a bolt from the blue. I remember one time we were playing Northants. I was not out overnight at the end of the first day but just as we were leaving the field after the morning work-out, I started to get the symptoms of a real king-size migraine.

It's not easy to describe but before the headache really kicks in, I develop tunnel vision, a bit like looking down one of those old kids' kaleidoscopes with violent colours and patterns everywhere. After a while, people and objects just turn into a shadowy blur – people like fast bowlers; objects like a cricket ball propelled at over 80 mph.

Looking back, I should have withdrawn from the fray as soon as the attack started. But we needed runs and I reckoned I could get away with it before the headache laid me low. Never again. Facing a high-speed bowler is bad enough when you can see. When everything is a blur, it's no fun at all. I could vaguely make out big men running in from the far end and a small round object heading in my general direction. But not a lot more. I prodded and poked around for a few overs before I was put out of my misery and could return to the pit and a long lie-down. Needless to say, as I walked in, I heard one or two unfavourable comments about my performance. If they had only known!

And now I've dislocated a finger. It hurts like hell and I don't suppose anyone would blame me for taking a break. No chance. By tradition, Yorkshire wicketkeepers hang around for a long time and I am following in a very illustrious line. Arthur Wood played in 408 first-class matches between 1927 and 1946 and since the War, the principal keepers have been Jimmy Binks, who played in 491 matches including a run of 412 consecutive Championship games, and David Bairstow, who made 429 first-class appearances.

So far, I've totted up 277 and if I can hang together until the end of the season I will be up to 283, with 121 consecutive appearances since August, 1992. But as we only play 17 games a season (and it will be 16 next year) compared to over 30 in Binks's day and around 25 for most of Bairstow's career, I'll need at least another seven seasons to reach the 400 mark. Still, I live in hope – and I'm damned if a dislocated finger is going to stop me.

CGU National League, Scarborough. 25 July. Yorkshire 178 (A. McGrath 68) lost to Kent 179–7 by 3 wickets.

LANCASHIRE V YORKSHIRE, OLD TRAFFORD. NATWEST TROPHY QUARTER-FINAL

Tuesday, 28 July. They simply do not come any bigger than this. Yorkshire's season will be on a knife-edge tomorrow when they take on their Roses rivals. Defeat would undermine their entire campaign and they come to Old Trafford acutely aware that they have lost three semi-finals on this ground in the last eight years, two of them in 1996. Lancashire, the acknowledged kings of the one-day game in recent years, have not lost a NatWest Trophy tie here since 1987, a sequence of eight straight wins. The Yorkshire players, confidence undermined by three successive National League defeats, arrive in Manchester on the eve of the match. They are expecting a strenuous work-out. Instead coach Martyn Moxon orders them back to the team hotel on the outskirts of the city with instructions to 'relax and enjoy yourselves. Have a lazy afternoon.' It could prove a masterstroke.

No complaints from me about an afternoon off. An ideal opportunity to finish off my *Huddersfield Examiner* column and fax it off to the sports desk ready for tomorrow's paper, well ahead of the deadline for a change. More important, the finger is still extremely sore and a couple of hours' practice would only have made things worse. Instead I was able to keep applying the icepacks – but I know only too well that it's not going to be a party when the action starts tomorrow.

Martyn arranged a team meeting at the hotel for 5.45 p.m., and we were all given an opportunity to have a say about what's been going wrong lately. It was undoubtedly the frankest meeting I have ever attended. Usually the lads are understandably reluctant to criticise other members of the team for their contribution, but not this time. It was honest, heart-to-heart stuff and no one ducked any issues. We looked long and hard at every individual's performance and the general team effort, particularly the fielding which has been well below par lately.

All the players joined in and some forthright opinions about how individuals have not been coming up to scratch in the last fortnight were exchanged. It never actually got heated but people were able to get things off their chest. And by the time we left after an hour of straight talking, the boys were far more relaxed and upbeat.

And we won't be letting speculation about the state of the pitch affect our approach. There's been a lot of talk in the papers about the Old Trafford square. Apparently Lancashire have run out of pitches and this match will be played on a track that was used for a World Cup game about six weeks ago.

Another old pitch was pressed into action for the recent televised day-night game between Lancashire and Warwickshire and it turned out to be an absolute nightmare. The TV pundits were dropping fifty pence pieces down cracks on a length and sure enough in the few overs before rain halted play, the ball was rearing all over the place.

Yorkshire supporters have been taking one look at a Lancashire line-up boasting the world-class talents of Sri Lanka spinner Muttiah Muralitharan and crying foul. They fear we will be playing on Old Trafford's equivalent of Blackpool beach and Murali and their other spinners will be unplayable.

The players don't see it that way. To be quite honest, the whole rumpus has gone clean over my head. Players can't possibly allow such negative thoughts to creep in before a game of this stature. If we arrive at the ground thinking we'll be playing on a real turner, or a Bunsen as we call it, and that Murali will take us to the cleaners then we're beaten before a ball is bowled. The Lankies have never been averse to tweaking a pitch to their own advantage – nor has any other county for that matter – but I'd be very surprised to find myself on a sandpit this time. Maybe we'll have to wait until the

Championship game next month for that exciting prospect!

My own view is that the whole issue is a piece of king-size gamesmanship from the Lancastrians. They're worried about us and they are trying to sow seeds of doubt in our minds by sending out warning signals about this so-called rogue pitch. I didn't even bother having a look earlier but one or two of the lads did and they seem to think it will play OK. The bottom line is that we need to go out there and play better than they do on the day, whatever the state of the pitch. Forget the hype, we've a job to do and we'll go and do it.

I just hope that tomorrow's surface gives both sides a chance to reproduce the kind of classic cup-tie we played in that Benson semi-final three years ago back in the bad old days when Lancashire exercised a huge psychological stranglehold over us. Tomorrow we intend to demonstrate that it is now a thing of the past.

Looking back, we were completely over-hyped for that game. We must have had half a dozen team meetings between our quarter-final win over Surrey on 28 May and arriving at Old Trafford on 11 June. It was team meetings about team meetings, team meals, team everything. This was going to be the big one.

It was pissing down with rain at the scheduled start and there was no way we should have started at all. But it was on the telly and there were over 16,000 people in the ground so play finally got under way at 4.30 p.m. After losing the toss and being put in, we found ourselves struggling along at 83 for 5 in next to no time.

It looked like the same old story of Yorkshire blowing it on the big occasion and when I went out to join Michael Bevan, the situation looked very dodgy. But this was the innings when I first realised what a marvellous one-day player and what a tough competitor Bevan is. With him around there's no such thing as a lost cause and by the close we were handily placed on 198 for 5 from 46 overs. The following morning we added another 52 in four overs. I closed on 80 and Bev, who had played one of the great Yorkshire one-day knocks and richly deserved a century, finished on 95 off 75 balls. It was an innings of the highest class and a staging point on his journey to becoming arguably the best one-day batsman in the world.

Our total of 250 for 5 left Lancashire with a mountain to climb and psychologically we were in the driving seat. When they still needed 77 off eight overs with only three wickets standing, we were already on the coach to Lord's. Then the wheels came off. Looking back we were so naïve. It never occurred to us that we might lose it and even though Lancashire crept nearer and nearer, we never really changed things around, tried anything different.

Our slow left-armer Richard Stemp, who has now moved on to play for Notts, had one over left to bowl and Gary Yates hammered the first two balls for six. Instead of switching to over the wicket or firing in a quicker delivery, in fact anything different, Stempy just kept looping the ball up and the over went for 20-plus. Lancashire were right back in it.

Then it was White versus Warren Hegg. Chalkie kept bowling to get him out, Hegg kept stepping back and hitting him inside out over cover for four. Like Stemp, Craig didn't try to vary it, to bounce him or go round the wicket. He just kept firing it in, looking for the wicket ball.

But even though the runs were flowing, we still never gave defeat a thought. Ten an over? No chance. With one over to go, eight to win, I was still convinced we would do it. So was everyone else. Glenn Chapple hit the first ball for four. Five balls, four to win; we'll still do it. A single, a wide, two dot balls. One ball to go, two to win and they still weren't going to get them. They did.

We learned the hard way all right. There were so many things that we got wrong that day. We just went with the flow instead of trying to dictate. If we had our chance all over again, it would be a different story. Who knows, tomorrow might be the day. And I promise you that if it goes down to the wire once more, you won't see the same naïve approach from this Yorkshire side. We've grown up. Afterwards, those eleven Yorkshire players were totally gutted. I have never known a dressing-room like it. No one could speak for half an hour. We were completely deflated and we never, ever want to go through anything like that again.

With the passage of time, I can look back and say that it was a wonderful game of cricket, a match that had absolutely everything. Ideally we'll give tomorrow's full house another last-ball thriller – with Yorkshire winning this time. But on reflection, I'll take a nine-wicket win with ten overs to spare.

Wednesday, 28 July. It wasn't quite that easy. But Yorkshire did end the hoodoo at last with a 55-run win. White, true to expectations, won the Gold Award for a blistering innings of 43 from 39 balls and a superb spell of seam bowling that earned him two wickets for 24 from eight overs. Byas, Vaughan, McGrath and Hamilton built the partnerships as planned and the unlikely bowling hero was Blewett. After Silverwood had broken a threatening third-wicket partnership of 90 between Michael Atherton and Neil Fairbrother by bowling Fairbrother, Blewett took over. His first delivery removed Atherton, and a huge heave by Andrew Flintoff gave him another victim, leg before three balls later. The Australian then ran out Hegg with a direct hit and after Blakey had run out Lloyd with another direct hit, Blewett claimed the last two wickets to finish with four for 18 from 5.4 overs. It was Lancashire's first NatWest defeat at Old Trafford since 1987.

Mission accomplished! At the start of the season, we had two monkeys on our back: one, Yorkshire had not played in a Lord's final for 12 years and cracked under pressure in the big semi-finals; two, when the chips were down, we couldn't beat Lancashire in a one-dayer at Old Trafford. In the space of 18 days, we have put both those jinxes down the waste disposal unit. We handled the pressure far better than Warwickshire to win the Super Cup semi-final at Edgbaston and now we have totally outplayed Lancashire in front of an Old Trafford full house.

We knew in advance exactly what we were trying to achieve. And we went out there and did the business. The batsmen played it to perfection, the bowlers never wavered and the fielding was excellent throughout. Not even the most partisan Lancastrian would deny that we outplayed them. We kept going, our heads never went down and we won it well in the end. The only mystery left is why we have blown so hot and cold in one-day cricket this season.

Who knows, this may be the turning point and we will start to put together some consistent displays. There's certainly enough at stake! Starting with the Super Cup final on Sunday, we have four one-dayers that could make or break the season because our next three National League games are against Worcestershire, the leaders, and, yes, Lancashire in two day-nighters home and away.

This win can only be a massive boost for us. Old Trafford has been a Red Rose fortress for so long that people have been saying we aren't psychologically strong enough to beat Lancashire on their own ground. We now know we can; a very big step forward for the team. Things are looking good.

The finger? On the morning of the game it was pretty damn sore to the touch. I only batted for an over at the end of the innings so there was little chance of further damage but I was still worried about when it came to keeping wicket.

I don't normally go in for painkillers because, as I have said before, they only mask an injury and there's no real way of knowing what the long-term after-effects may be. But in this instance I was assured that they would help ease what is a temporary problem. Before I put the gloves on I put as much padding as I could around the finger and then taped my two middle fingers together to try and provide more protection.

Despite the painkillers, I could feel it a bit even before a ball was bowled. But once the adrenaline kicked in, the pain was nothing more than a nagging discomfort. The lads did me a lot of favours with some excellent throwing, although on the one or two occasions when I had to take the ball on the half-volley, it sent a searing pain up my arm.

In the end, I came through, though, and the team won. That's all that matters. As a wicketkeeper, my hands are vital, to put it mildly, and it's uncomfortable knowing in the back of your mind that you have a problem. I didn't make a big deal of it with the rest of the boys because a few of them are carrying niggles, too, and they have enough on their plate trying to get through their own game. The last thing they are going to want is a doubt about the fitness of their wicketkeeper.

OK, it's bound to be a bit sore in the morning. But the good news is that it's responding to treatment and by the time we cross the starting line at Lord's on Sunday it should be more or less 100 per cent.

NatWest Trophy quarter-final, Old Trafford. 28 July. Yorkshire 263–7 (D. Byas 72, A. McGrath 60) beat Lancashire 208 (G.S. Blewett 4–18) by 55 runs.

YORKSHIRE V GLOUCESTERSHIRE, LORD'S. BENSON & HEDGES SUPER CUP FINAL

Friday, 30 July. Yorkshire have arranged a Press call at Headingley before the players leave for London. Once again, it's Yorkshire Tea and Betty's cakes all round as the local media focuses on Yorkshire's first Lord's final for 12 years. As the only survivor from the 1987 Benson & Hedges final win over Northants, Blakey is one of the main attractions, conducting press and television interviews before taking part in a live radio programme.

White and Blewett, the heroes of Wednesday's triumph at Old Trafford, are also much in demand as are Hamilton and Silverwood, both strongly tipped for an England call this weekend. Ryan Sidebottom, too – his dad Arnie was a team-mate of Blakey in that 1987 line-up. And as the camera shutters whirr, Byas, hoping to follow in the footsteps of Brian Close and Phil Carrick and become only the third Yorkshire captain to hoist the silverware aloft at Lord's, conducts seven radio, television and press interviews.

Over the course of a season, the Yorkshire players are, for the most part, a media-friendly bunch and not surprisingly, given the no-nonsense approach of their captain, there is a conspicuous absence of prima donnas.

So, on a glorious July morning, they happily bask in the reflected glory of Old Trafford and look ahead to an even more exciting horizon at Lord's. The atmosphere is informal and relaxed. Some would say too relaxed. And while none of the players are under-estimating Gloucestershire, there is definitely a feeling at Headingley this morning that Yorkshire's hour has come at last. Yorkshire's day on Yorkshire Day.

Even though the Super Cup has been pooh-poohed by many pundits, the Yorkshire public have responded enthusiastically to the first White Rose appearance in a Lord's final for more than a decade. One or two fans have even arrived at Headingley today, the younger generation in search of autographs, their seniors content to survey the scene in eager anticipation of triumph ahead. Trains and coaches are booked up, plans have been made for a weekend in the capital and, as ever in White Rose territory, expectations are sky-high. As Mark Newton, the marketing director enthuses, 'It's going to be a great day out.' We shall see.

The question I have been asked over and over again since we qualified for the final is: 'So, Richard, what are your memories of the 1987 Lord's victory?' As I'm the only member of Phil Carrick's side who is still around, it's understandable that the press, radio, television and supporters should be interested in me all of a sudden. And as I've always been a strong believer in speaking to the media and the fans, I've been more than happy to oblige.

The cards and good luck messages that have been flooding in since we qualified for the final demonstrate how much this game means to people in the county. I've hardly been off the phone all week – no, not friends wanting tickets, just well-wishers hoping we go down there and bring back the cup. I'm sure people outside the county don't appreciate the cricketing fervour that still exists here and as a member of the last Yorkshire side to win anything, I'm suddenly the focus of attention.

Just one problem, though. I can't really remember too much about that famous last-ball victory over Northants 12 years ago. I took a catch to dismiss Geoff Cook off Paul Jarvis early on and scored just one run after Martyn Moxon and Ashley Metcalfe had started our pursuit of 245 from 55 overs with an opening stand of 97. I can remember Arnie Sidebottom bringing the scores level off the penultimate ball and Jim Love, knowing he only had to survive the final delivery from Winston Davis to give Yorkshire the cup on fewer wickets lost, blocking it out. Some of the players couldn't bear to watch that last ball; others were out on the balcony, biting their nails, unable to speak because of the tension. Me? I never had any doubts. We were going to win. Oh, the innocence of youth!

I can remember going out on to the main balcony afterwards, receiving my medal and joining in the celebrations as Carrick hoisted the cup aloft. And I can recall the sheer delight on the faces of the senior players who had spent most of their careers waiting for this moment, Yorkshire's first Lord's trophy since 1969. But the rest of the day is a bit of blur.

And so, needless to say, are the celebrations. The fixture planners can't have thought we would be involved in the B&H final when they made out the 1987 programme because the day after the Lord's match we were scheduled to play Middlesex up at Scarborough. Their captain Mike Gatting was the Man of the Match adjudicator for the final so, with the party already in full swing, we scooped up Gatt, climbed aboard the team bus and headed off up the motorway to overnight at the Selby Fork Motel on the A1 before going on to North Marine Road the next morning.

Did I say overnight? I don't think anyone on the trip slept a wink – including Gatt. On the way up north, the champagne was flowing, so was the beer. Anyone brave enough to venture down the aisle ended up with his socks soaked in a combination of Moët et Chandon and Tetley Bitter. When we arrived in Selby the party stepped up a couple of gears yet by some miracle we were all back on the coach next morning and off to the seaside. Somewhere at the back of our minds was the recollection that we had a game of cricket to play.

There was a huge crowd at North Marine Road and we were cheered all the way down the track from the main entrance to the pavilion. And then out into the middle. We played on auto pilot and somehow contrived to give Middlesex a good hiding, winning by 33 runs. As it happened, I didn't play regularly in the Sunday League that season, so I was able to take it easy in a darkened dressing-room. Afterwards it was up on to the balcony to raise the cup once again to a standing ovation from the whole crowd. And then the party started all over again.

I was just 20 and halfway through my first full season as a Yorkshire player after making my début two years earlier. The runs were flowing and as I mentioned earlier I did well enough to win the Cricket Writers' award for the Young Player of the Year. The world was a marvellous place, cricket was a wonderful, easy game and reaching a Lord's final was just another experience to be collected along the way. As far as I was concerned Yorkshire would be winning trophies and I would be scoring runs for another 20 years and I simply never appreciated the magnitude of what was going on around me.

But if I had imagined for a split second that it would be 12 years before I would be back I might have taken a bit more notice. I would have absorbed more of a great cricketing occasion.

It's going to be a very different story this time, though. I am going to savour every moment of the experience. Yes, even if we lose. I am confident that we'll lift the cup and I'm also confident that we'll be back at Lord's for the NatWest Trophy final at the end of August, although ironically we'll have to beat our Super Cup opponents Gloucestershire in the semi-final first.

On Sunday, I'll take time out to wander out on to the dressing-room balcony before we start our warm-up and have a look around a deserted Lord's. I'll make sure I watch the ground filling up, I'll make a mental note of the journey through the long room, down the pavilion steps and out on to the playing area. As I walk out to the middle, I'll drink in the atmosphere. And when it's all over, win or lose, and we've collected our medals, I'll try and find a quiet moment out on the balcony as the sun goes down behind the stands. I suppose the kids in the team will think I'm a sentimental old fool and I probably thought the same about Carrick, Bairstow, Arnie and Co. all those years ago. But it's my turn to be 32 now – and you never know, I might not be back.

Sunday, 1 August, Yorkshire Day. The Super Cup final is a disaster. Gloucestershire, led by their captain Mark Alleyne, batter the Yorkshire attack into submission with a total of 291 for 9 from their 50 overs. Yorkshire finish 124 runs short after a poor exhibition of batting that occupies just 40 of their overs allocation.

No excuses – a bitterly disappointing day. I kept my promise to sit on the balcony for a few quiet minutes afterwards, and seeing all the Yorkshire supporters trudging away while the Gloucester players and their fans celebrated made me feel so sorry. They had spent good money to come and enjoy a special occasion; a lot of them stayed overnight in London and they came to Lord's in their thousands to see us win – or at the very least put up a decent show. But we just didn't perform. We let ourselves down and we let our supporters down.

From the moment David lost the toss it was downhill all the way. The bowlers didn't find a consistent line and length, the fielding was below par and we went in at half-time facing a total of 291 for 9 and the odds stacked heavily against us. The atmosphere in the dressing-room was horribly subdued. We had to get away to a good start with something like 100 for not many on the board after the first 15 overs but instead we lost early wickets and the rest is history. A victory by 124 runs tells its own story. We were outplayed and it hurt.

I've known Mark Alleyne since we played for England Schools together in the early '80s and he's a decent bloke. He played marvellously well for his century, although our bowlers helped him along the way. But standing behind him on the balcony as he raised the cup aloft was a sickening moment. It could have been David Byas with the trophy and our fans down there cheering.

Inevitably, the old theory about Yorkshire bottling out when the stakes are high will rear its ugly head. I don't go along with that. We didn't funk it in the semi-final against Warwickshire at Edgbaston. We didn't blow up in the Old Trafford cauldron just four days ago. In those games we proved to everyone – and above all to ourselves – that we can hack it when the chips are down. But here at Lord's we just played badly. It's as simple as that.

Sometimes, though, in one-day cricket we're victims of our own success. We've produced this battery of high-speed pace bowlers who can be a formidable proposition on their day. But never forget the old adage about the faster the ball flies, the further it goes. And these guys pay a high price for any error in line or length.

After we played Warwickshire in the National League a couple of weeks ago, one or two of the lads were saying that Allan Donald had been the easiest of their bowlers to score runs against – and he's just about the fastest bowler in the world. He's devastating at Test match or

Championship level when an edge almost inevitably means a catch to the slip cordon. But in one-day games, the field is spread far and wide and if he isn't right on the spot, batsmen can have a dart at him with a reasonable chance of getting away with it.

Our next National League opponents are Worcestershire and their attack is particularly useful in limited overs cricket. There's no express pace but people like Tom Moody, David Leatherdale and Stuart Lampitt can nag away with the keeper standing up and really make a batsman work for his runs. Believe me, I'm not making excuses for a poor performance – but that is a genuine reason why we sometimes go for a lot of runs in one-day cricket. And we sure as hell went for a few in front of 20,000 fans at Lord's.

From an individual standpoint, when I went to the crease to join Gavin Hamilton we were 122 for 6 in the 28th over, still needing 170 from 22. Impossible? Probably. But in this game, you never give it away. After all, Bevan and I took 50 from four overs against Lancashire in that semi-final three years ago. Gav and I talked it through. Their spinners, Martyn Ball and Jeremy Snape, were operating in tandem and we decided to try and nudge it around at six or seven an over before having a real thrash when the seamers returned. By then the asking rate would be up over ten. OK, a shot in the dark but at least we had a plan to follow.

They bowled tight and while we managed to keep the runs ticking over we were always under the cosh and the pressure was tightening all the time with the asking rate moving sky-high. We had added 34 in seven overs when I missed a straight one, as they say, and was bowled by Ball for 14. Gavin followed soon afterwards and it was game, set and match. Disappointing, though, to hear some of our fans having a go at us for not trying to turn some of those singles into twos.

I don't know how it looked from the sidelines but I've played over 500 games for Yorkshire and I know how it feels to be out there in the middle in a situation like that. With all due respect to the barrackers, they simply haven't a clue. The plan Gav and I had worked out was our best chance of winning the match for Yorkshire and with seven wickets down, you do not – repeat not – chance your arm on a dodgy second run. I can imagine what the response would have been if Hamilton or I had run ourselves out or been bowled giving it the charge with 15 overs or so still to be bowled.

I've taken my share of criticism from the fans down the years and they're entitled to their opinions. I would never deny that. But in this instance I was acting in what I genuinely believed were the best interests of Yorkshire cricket. That has always been my approach to the game, and it always will be.

So, we lost a cricket match; a very important cricket match. Afterwards, it felt like the end of the world. But it isn't. Life goes on, cricket goes on. We live to fight another day – and one of those days, don't forget, is a NatWest semi-final against Gloucester at Bristol in two weeks.

Apart from the skipper, who had to talk to the media afterwards, no one in the dressing-room moved for an hour or so. We just couldn't be bothered getting changed and going back to the team hotel for what should have been a night of celebrations with our folks. But after a beer on the coach, some of the disappointment started to drain away. We went out for a few drinks afterwards and now we're on the long, tired journey back to Headingley. We'll be glad to get home. But if anyone thinks this defeat has knocked the stuffing out of Yorkshire cricket, they can think again. We play Worcester in the Championship on Wednesday and we'll be up for that one, make no mistake about that.

B&H Super Cup final, Lord's. 1 August. Yorkshire 167 lost to Gloucestershire 291–9 (M.W. Alleyne 112, R.J. Cunliffe 61, C. White 4–51) by 124 runs.

YORKSHIRE V WORCESTERSHIRE, HEADINGLEY

Wednesday, 4 August. After the bitter disappointment of Lord's, Yorkshire return home for a vital Championship game against Worcestershire. Even though they are in sixth place in the table, they are by no means in the comfort zone and just four points above tenth place and Second Division cricket next season. No way to start the new millennium. They take on Worcester without three members of their pace attack. Darren Gough and Matthew Hoggard will not play again this season because of injury and Chris Silverwood has again been called up by England for the Third Test against New Zealand at Old Trafford. And worries about the batting persist, particularly the team's inability to make a decent start. They have passed 50 for the first wicket only twice all season and have yet to record a century opening stand. Ironically, Yorkshire once scored 351 for the first wicket against today's opponents. But that was a long time ago – 1985 to be precise, in Blakey's first season of Championship cricket. The openers involved were Martyn Moxon and a certain Geoffrey Boycott.

Boycott. Now there's a name to conjure with. Probably more words have been written about Sir Geoffrey than any other cricketer on the planet. But I can confidently wager that no one outside a highly select band of former Yorkshire cricketers will share my abiding memory of Boycott: the day he was hurled into a bath full of ice-cold water – in Hull, of all places.

It was back in 1984 when I was sweet 17 and just making my way in the Second XI along with such luminaries as Ian Swallow, Paul Booth, Stuart Fletcher, all fellow Huddersfield League products, Chris Pickles, Chris Shaw and Steve Rhodes, now Worcestershire's wicketkeeper, of course. Now it just so happened that Boycs, who was 44 at the time but still Yorkshire's leading batsman, was on the way back from injury and had asked for a work-out with the Seconds. He scored a century. Naturally.

Little did he realise, though, that encounters inside his own dressing-room were going to be far tougher than anything he would face out in the middle. In those days, the Yorkshire Second XI contained some pranksters of rare quality, none more so than Ian Swallow, who later moved to Somerset and these days is still one of the best league cricketers around. And as soon as the news broke that Boycs would be playing at The Circle, Swallow, or Chicken George as we sometimes called him, started to plot his downfall.

Now the pavilion at The Circle was like some rickety old mansion, full of dark corridors with doors leading off to all sorts of weird and wonderful places. The showers and baths were through one of these doors and down a flight of steps. You half expected to see someone emerge from the after-match ablutions with a shovelful of coal. So while Boycott was out in the middle, caressing his way back to form and fitness, Swall struck. Just before the close of play, he filled one of the baths with cold water, urging one of the lads to fetch all the available ice cubes from the bar. That was added to the brew.

Geoffrey eventually returned to the pavilion after a demonstration of, to use his own well-worn phrase, technique and concentration and proceeded to go through his undressing routine. There was a place for everything in the Boycott bag and his kit was always in immaculate condition and scrupulously inspected before it was put away. Eventually, when he was finally bollock-naked and ready for a well-deserved refreshing shower, Swallow pounced. Boycott found himself pinioned to the floor by six pairs of hands, lifted aloft, carried down the stairs and, protesting vehemently, chucked into the bath. We made our escape to the relative safety of the dressing-room accompanied by roars of anger from England's premier batsman. 'You bastards, you fucking bastards. I'll get the bloody lot of you. One by one! Just you fucking wait!' He always had a choice turn of phrase, did Boycs.

Needless to say, all the lads in the dressing-room were howling with laughter, wondering how Geoffrey would respond. We didn't have long to wait. Down in the cellar was a mop and bucket that the cleaners used to mop up after we'd all gone home. And the contents of the bucket were truly disgusting. It was only emptied once every Preston Guild and there was all sorts of gunge in the bottom that had accumulated down the years. As soon as we heard the clang of the bucket, we knew what Boycott's revenge would be. He had correctly pinpointed the ringmaster and after topping up the bucket from the bath, came thundering upstairs, shouting 'Right, Swallow, this is for you, you Chicken George bastard!'

Now Ian hadn't achieved his status as chief prankster without being able to think fast. And it just so happened that Geoffrey was due to attend an official function that night and had brought his best suit, shirt and tie along. Swallow moved like lightning in the few minutes available before his assailant burst into the room. Geoffrey quickly identified his target and the aim was true. But it wasn't until the contents of the bucket were in mid-air that he realised Ian was wearing the Boycott shirt. And if you thought the language was bad before, you should have heard him as he surveyed the wreckage.

To his credit, Boycs soon saw the funny side of it and exerted his considerable influence to beg, borrow or steal a replacement shirt. What we couldn't understand in the immediate aftermath was why he left for his dinner looking decidedly smug and sporting that familiar lopsided grin. It was only when we were all dressed and ready for a night out of our own that we realised why. Earlier in the day, Boycott had volunteered to lock all our wallets in his car boot for safe keeping. And they were still safely tucked away in there as his luxury limo disappeared into the middle distance. No doubt all the guests at that particular dinner still comment about Sir Geoffrey's enormous generosity.

Little did I know as I contemplated a singularly uneventful evening that 12 months later, I would be in the same Yorkshire side as Boycott. He wasn't playing when I made my début against Middlesex in the opening game of the 1985 reason and for some reason, which I have never been able to work out, the innings was opened by Arnie Sidebottom, a fast bowler good enough to win an England cap but hardly in Geoffrey's class with the bat. But over the next few months I spent a lot of time at the crease and in the dressing-room with The Master.

It's no secret that he was not universally popular among his team-mates, particularly some of the senior players, and the rifts and rancour within the Yorkshire side at the time have been well-documented elsewhere. I have tried, in this book, to avoid commenting on issues in which I have not been directly involved and these include the problems in the Yorkshire camp before I became a regular member of the side in 1987, by which time Boycs had finally retired with 48,426 first-class runs to his name, at an average of more than 50. But in those first two seasons I could sense an atmosphere in the dressing-room between Boycott and the senior players.

Personally, though, I have always had a tremendous amount of time for Geoffrey on and off the field. I'm a firm believer that you can only take people as you find them and you will never hear me say a wrong word about Boycs. When I was a kid, playing in the back garden, I would always be Boycott. As I progressed into the first team at Elland in the Huddersfield League and played for Yorkshire and England Schools, I copied his technique. He was my role model.

So I was inevitably a bit overawed to find myself in the same dressing-room. At least he seemed to know who I was – unlike Paul Booth when he made his début at Scarborough a few years earlier. In those days, there was no such thing as kit sponsorship and players used to turn up and play for Yorkshire in their club gear. Booth, a useful left-arm spinner who also played for Warwickshire and is now in the same Huddersfield League side as his old pal Swallow, was wearing a Meltham CC sweater hand-knitted by his mum. Boycott thought he was one of the ground staff lads and kept asking him to run errands. It wasn't until they trotted out on to the field together that he realised his mistake.

I had a good relationship with Boycott from the start. He had a reputation for being reluctant to give advice but I soon found the opposite was true. OK, if we were in the nets, he wouldn't come over and volunteer a few tips. But all you had to do was ask him to help you out and he would spare as much time as you wanted.

The down side was that he expected everyone to share his high standards and as far as batting technique was concerned, that meant perfection. And perfection is a hard act to follow. But he was always ready to help me out and I remember meeting him at Wortley Golf Club near Sheffield before setting off on the England A tour to Zimbabwe in 1990. Listening to him was like having a master class in batting. Perhaps it's no coincidence that I topped the tour averages with 337 runs at an average of 84.25 and made my highest first-class score of 221. His knowledge of every aspect of the game is phenomenal.

I played in about 15 matches with him during that first season and it was a privilege to be 22 yards away at the other end of the wicket. Even though his best years were behind him, his technique was almost flawless and his concentration immense. He lived in a bubble of his own.

I can also boast to be one of his few Yorkshire contemporaries that he never ran out, although he tried bloody hard in one game at Scarborough at the end of the 1985 season. He must have been in good nick because he was clipping a single off the last ball of just about every over, leaving me to admire his progress from the other end. Sure enough, ball number six of this particular over came down, Boycs nudged it to mid-wicket and called me through for the single. It was never really on, though, and we went through the full array of yes, no, wait, maybe, during which time I ran three while he never left the crease!

I've always enjoyed his company and make a point of popping into the commentary box whenever he's around. Last season, he agreed to do a chat show with Michael Parkinson as part of my Benefit Year. It was held at Huddersfield Town Hall and the evening was due to start at 7.30 p.m. When the star turns had not arrived by 7.20, even the normally laid-back Richard Blakey was starting to fray at the edges, wondering how to keep 800 irate Yorkshiremen happy without giving them their money back. The town hall PR girl put it bluntly: 'They're not coming, are they?' I assured her they would be and asked, as a matter of interest, what time people normally arrived for these functions. 'Quarter to seven,' she replied.

At that moment, a car swept up, out hopped Boycs and Parky and after a quick glass of water in the hospitality suite, they gave the performance of their lives that had the audience enthralled from the moment Parky asked his first question. And all for my Benefit.

And how Worcestershire could have used Boycott's legendary application and ability against the moving ball. His 'concentration and technique.' After winning the toss and electing to bat on a bright sunny Headingley morning, they are bowled out for 90. Paul Hutchison, playing his first Championship game of the summer, leads the way as Yorkshire, showing the better side of their nature, start to put the memory of that Lord's defeat behind them.

An excellent toss to lose. A nice morning, the pitch looked good and any skipper calling correctly would have chosen to bat. Tom Moody did exactly that – and we prepared for a long day in the field. Instead the ball swung round corners and we bowled them out for 90 before lunch on the first morning. Understandably, their heads went down, the pitch dried out in the afternoon, Bingo and Virgil made decent scores and we lead by 284 on first innings. Game over.

Gavin Hamilton underlined his growing batting prowess with an undefeated 94, his highest first class score. I helped him add 62 for the seventh wicket and desperately wanted to be there when he reached three figures, only to get out when I had made 22. And the remaining batsmen didn't last long. Gav was disappointed of course – but his day will come.

The performance of the whole side was a tremendous way to bounce back from the defeat at Lord's and sent out a message that we haven't given up on any of the three remaining trophies yet. Not by a long way.

Hutchison, playing his first Championship game after finally recovering from the back problem that forced him home from last winter's A tour, did the damage, taking six wickets for 35. It's good to have him back. With Goughie and Matthew Hoggard ruled out long term and Gavin still feeling his hamstring, Hutch's return has beefed up our bowling strength significantly. He's a class act. To say he hasn't played a Championship game all year, he bowled a great line and length and troubled all the batsmen with his movement through the air.

It's obviously a huge disappointment that we've had so many injury problems but I would hate that to sound like an excuse for some of our below-par performances. Because even without Darren, Paul and Matthew, all of whom would probably feature in a first choice attack, we have been able to field Chris Silverwood and Ryan Sidebottom as pace bowlers with Craig White and Gavin as fast bowling all-rounders. So we're not exactly short of quality – and the whole thinking behind having such a strong squad is that injuries and Test calls will not matter. Instead the bowlers, like the batters, have not performed well enough, often enough.

Having said that, though, the absence of Hoggie and Hutch has removed some variety from the attack. Both swing the ball a lot and swing it late and it doesn't matter how flat a pitch is, bowlers will take wickets if they swing the ball through the air. And Matthew has that extra yard of pace as well. When he was right on top of his form at the end of last season he was a formidable proposition. I thought I would get a catch every ball.

This season I fully expected him to progress from a promising, raw seamer to the fully fledged article. He started well and looked set for a high quality year until picking up this knee injury. He's had surgery and may reappear at the end of the season but realistically he'll be looking to have another good winter in South African domestic cricket and then be fit to return for us in 2000.

PPP Healthcare County Championship, Headingley. 4–7 August. Yorkshire 374 (G.M. Hamilton 94*) and 4–1 beat Worcestershire 90 (P.M. Hutchison 6–35) and 287 (V. Solanki 70) by 9 wickets.

YORKSHIRE PHOENIX V WORCESTERSHIRE ROYALS, HEADINGLEY. NATIONAL LEAGUE

Sunday, 8 August. A Headingley crowd of over 12,000 gathers for a potentially decisive National League game against Worcester Royals, who have taken over the First Division leadership during Yorkshire Phoenix's collapse that has seen them slump to defeat in each of their last three games. With two day-night games against third-placed Lancashire to follow in the next nine days, Yorkshire cannot afford to lose again. A year ago Blakey, in the throes of his Benefit Year, would have surveyed the scene of a packed Headingley with surprisingly mixed feelings.

To be honest, I always found the sound of cash dropping into the collection buckets a bit embarrassing. I didn't really know how to respond. On the one hand, I wanted to show some kind of acknowledgement, let the people who were supporting me know how much I appreciated it; on the other hand, I was acutely aware that people were being asked to dip into their pockets on my behalf and I would rather have taken refuge in somewhere less exposed than the middle of a cricket field until the collection was complete. Difficult.

For the record my Benefit Year raised over a hundred and twenty thousand pounds, more or less tax free, and I cannot say thank you often enough to all the thousands of people who contributed or who helped in any way. It's a lot of money and if I use it sensibly I can give myself some security for the rest of my life.

But cricketers don't earn a fortune. Apart from all the top international players, we are not well paid, although players are free to negotiate their own deals, of course. For six months' work, it's decent pay and taken overall, it's a great life. But employment can be hard to find in the winter and our wages will never be enough to retire on when we finish playing.

So the Benefit system is a way of rewarding a professional for ten or more years' service with one club. It's a thank you, if you like, from the club and its supporters for loyal service. I've no problem with that. A good, honest pro who has slogged away through thick and thin down the years, deserves something out of the game as he nears the end of his career.

Having said that, a Benefit Year really is a very tough and stressful time. I lost count of the number of fall-outs I had with my partner Clare – and all the time, she was one of the people helping to make the year such a success. The number of times she donned the Dickie Dog mascot's costume was certainly above and beyond the call of duty.

I seemed to spend most of the year either on the road, on the telephone or writing and answering letters. Somewhere along the line I had to find time to play some cricket and managed to go through the season without missing a single game. In an ideal world, the beneficiary would be able to sit back, relax and enjoy every minute but I can't think of many players who have been able to do that. For most of us, it's a hectic year with a really tough schedule.

As well as big dinners all over the county there were cricket matches, golf days, sports forums, race days and all sorts of other activities like the evening in Huddersfield with Michael Parkinson and Geoffrey Boycott. And I received support from people in all walks of life, from the business community to individual people who wanted to say more of a personal thank you by organising a function of their own.

That made the year a very humbling experience in many ways. I knew there would be events like the spectacular Christmas night at The McAlpine Stadium with 300 guests and Dermot Reeve as the main speaker. But when a lifelong Yorkshire cricket fan rings up to say how much he has always admired you and would like to arrange a Benefit match or an evening function, it is a moving experience. As a player, you accept that the punters are going to give you some stick. But you never quite expect your own little fan club to come out of the woodwork and start helping the Benefit cause. And I'm not ashamed to admit that some of the nice things that were said about me at little functions around the county brought a tear to my eye.

For my colleagues, the Benefit Year was a mixed blessing, to put it mildly. I've said earlier in the book how there are loads of occasions during the season when players drag themselves into bed late on a Sunday night after a long-haul match, just dreaming of a couple of days off to recharge the batteries before the next game. They need time to relax, time to do their own thing, time to pay the bills and sort out their personal affairs.

Instead I was asking them to chuck the gear in the car yet again and set off for a Benefit match in some remote part of the county against a group of amateur players. But they supported me right down to the wire and gave full value wherever they went. But they won't be sorry there isn't a beneficiary this year!

Looking back, my Benefit Year was incredibly hard work but, on balance, a rewarding experience. And I'm not just talking about the money. I made new friends, established new contacts and I can now look back and say what a good year it was.

The advantage of the Benefit system is that it gives a long-serving player an opportunity to plan for his retirement if he invests his money wisely. The downside is that there are a lot of players around who are not comfortable taking centre stage at social events, who are naturally shy and prefer to stay in the background. For them, the Benefit Year must be a nightmare and inevitably it is less successful. Is this fair? No. And maybe the authorities should consider setting up some kind of fund from which players take a lump sum, based on their years of service, when they retire. Whether it will ever come about, of course, remains to be seen.

As it happens, the Benefit buckets will be out again at Headingley today. This time the collection is in aid of a very different cause altogether, the Jamie Hood Appeal Fund. Jamie was on the threshold of a county career when, during an overseas professional engagement, he was involved in a car crash. He is now confined to a wheelchair. If anyone ever deserved a king-size collection, it's you Jamie.

The match ends in another sorry defeat for Yorkshire, their fourth in a row in a competition they threatened to dominate in the opening weeks of the season. Blewett's farewell appearance before linking up with the Australian squad for their tour of Sri Lanka ends, predictably perhaps, in failure. And the warning signals from a feeble performance suggest that Yorkshire's season, that opened with so many lofty hopes, is locked in a downward spiral.

A desperately poor performance. There was a massive crowd in to see the top two in the National League go head to head. Victory would have put us back in pole position and banished the memories of that below-par one-day display at Lord's seven days earlier. So, a very, very important game. I was fired up for it from the moment I woke up and when I arrived at the ground I expected to find our den really on fire. But no. There was absolutely no buzz about the team at all. We were completely flat.

It didn't help that Gavin Hamilton's hamstring went again after he had bowled 15 balls but I'd already been picking up all the wrong vibes before that injury happened. The first wicket fell when I caught Phil Weston off Silvers with the score at 28. After the celebrations, we went into a huddle in the middle of the wicket and the captain thundered, 'What the fuck's going on? You're second in the league, you're playing the leaders and you're like a side just going through the motions.'

I backed him up in similar vein. That's not normally my scene. I say my piece in the dressing-room, of course, but primarily I'm big on quieter forms of motivation out in the middle. Most of the bowlers are still young and learning the game and I see it as part of my job to keep having a word in the ear; a gee-up or a well done, keep it going. But on this occasion I wasn't getting through, I just couldn't understand what was happening. It felt like a meaningless end-of-season affair, not a crucial National League championship game. It really was bewildering.

It seemed the players had come down from a Lord's final and were resting up before a couple of big day-night games against Lancashire and an even bigger NatWest semi-final against Gloucester. We have worked hard on attitude all season but in this game there was nothing there at all. Bitterly disappointing.

Worcester progressed serenely to 228 for 7 from their 45 overs and when Gavin, batting with a runner, joined me at the crease at around the halfway mark of our reply, we were 95 for 7. We put on 48 and I top-scored with 30. But so what? We were all out for 143 and we had lost our fourth National League game in a row. Not only that, but we had lost by an overwhelming margin. I felt low and very disappointed in the pit afterwards.

Nobody was more unhappy than Greg Blewett about the result and our performance. Blewie wanted to go out on a high note but he concluded the worst season by any of our overseas players with just 24. I had a beer with him later and he is genuinely sorry not to be seeing out the campaign, even though he has had such a disastrous time. His four months here have been the most unproductive spell of his career from a personal point of view. He scored only 655 runs at an average of 31.19 in Championship games, including that 98 and 190 not out at Scarborough recently, and just 178 in the National League without reaching 50 once. Incomprehensible figures for a player of his class.

He doesn't make excuses but he admits the pitches over here have been far harder to bat on than he expected. And the balls we use have swung and seamed around more than the ball they use Down Under. By his own admission he's been out leg before and caught in the slips too often for a player of his calibre, a sure sign that he hasn't mastered the moving ball. But I have no doubt that he will emerge from this ordeal mentally tougher and technically better equipped to make England pay the next time the Aussies are over here.

As far as Yorkshire are concerned, though, the bottom line is that he came here to score big runs and win matches and hasn't come up with the goods. We've found ourselves pissing against the wind after losing early wickets far too often and his two big scores that saved the match against Northants came after he had dropped down the order. In fact, it's ironic that Blewie will be remembered most for *bowling* us to our victory in the NatWest Trophy quarter-final at Old Trafford.

CGU National League, Headingley. 8 August. Yorkshire Phoenix 143 (R.J. Blakey 30) lost to Worcestershire Royals 228–7 (T.M. Moody 56) by 85 runs.

YORKSHIRE PHOENIX V LANCASHIRE LIGHTNING, HEADINGLEY & OLD TRAFFORD. NATIONAL LEAGUE

Thursday, 12 August. Four successive National League defeats suggest that, for Yorkshire at least, Headingley's only day-night match of the season may be little more than an academic exercise in terms of Championship success. That will not be sufficient to deter a crowd of over 12,000 arriving to enjoy the spectacle of floodlit cricket. The traditionalists, for whom cricket's pyjama game is anathema, will not be among them. Even though Roses rivals Lancashire provide the opposition.

Day-night cricket? Count me in! I love it. And if you ask most of the players on the county circuit who have experienced cricket under the lights, I'm sure you'll get the same response.

Let's not mince words. Cricket has an image problem. The football season opened last weekend to massive coverage in every form of the media and huge crowds at the big Premiership games. At the same time, England were playing New Zealand in the third Test at Old Trafford in front of a pitifully small gathering.

I heard one report that there were more spectators at an ice hockey match in Manchester at the weekend than there were at the Test. And with all due respect, if that's true, cricket is in trouble. OK, we might not be able to compete with football in terms of attendances, but we must, and I mean must, do something to turn our image around.

I'm convinced day-night cricket is one of the answers – and I don't care how much that upsets the so-called traditionalist lobby who throw their hands up in horror at the sight of players in coloured clothing, a white ball, cheering and chanting fans and musical accompaniment for every boundary or wicket. They probably also turn away in disgust at the sight of cricket grounds packed with over 10,000 people, many of them young kids who have never been involved with the game before. But like it or not, they are cricket's future.

When we were down at Lord's the other week, I lost count of the number of youngsters I saw wearing Yorkshire Phoenix replica shirts and we have to go out and make sure those kids are not lost to the game. We can't just sit back and expect them to turn up; we have to do something positive to attract them.

Last year, Lancashire provided the opposition for Yorkshire's first home day-night game and the occasion was a huge success – apart from the result. They battered us by 101 runs and the fireworks that rounded off the proceedings were very much a damp squib as far as we were concerned. But it was a lovely summer's evening, there were over 12,000 people in the ground and polls taken at the time showed that a large percentage of them had never been to a cricket match before. That game triggered their imagination. It was a great spectacle and I guarantee most of them will be back for a second helping tonight.

A lot of them will be sporting their team's coloured clothing with the name of their favourite player on the back. And why not? Pyjamas, as the critics call them, are definitely part of the one-day razzmatazz and I would go all the way and play every one-day game in every competition in coloured clothing.

We played in another day-night game at Leicester earlier in the season and once again there was a super atmosphere. And after this game we have a third match under the lights against Lancashire at Old Trafford next week. This kind of cricket gives the players a buzz. It's bright, it's noisy, it's colourful, it's dynamic and instead of staring at rows of empty seats, you're playing in front of a near full house.

One-day cricket is the future. Like it or not, we are just another arm of the entertainment business and if people no longer enjoy the product we have to offer, we must change. As numbers continue to dwindle for the four-day game, day-night cricket is attracting a new army of spectators and we must hang on to them.

I can honestly foresee the day when we will play only one-day cricket at international and domestic level. It's a long way down the road and I don't believe for a minute that it will happen while I'm still playing. But if cricket's audience continues to change and people continue to turn their backs on the longer game and turn up in increasing numbers for one-day matches, then the road ahead is obvious.

The Yorkshire players had a marvellous week's cricket a fortnight ago. First we had that NatWest Trophy quarter-final at Old Trafford, complete with all the big build-up, the huge crowd and the tremendous atmosphere. It was a superb day. After three days to come down from the high and recharge the batteries, we were involved in another king-size match, this time a Lord's final in front of another big crowd. OK, we didn't play well and lost out on the day. But those are the kind of occasions players and supporters live for.

It's a different kind of cricket in front of a different kind of audience, of course. And some of the comments we hear out in the middle suggest that more than a few of the fans are not exactly in tune with the finer points of the game. But so what? They have paid good money to come and watch us and they are entitled to say what they think. And let's face it, not *every* comment from the members in a Championship match comes undistilled from the fount of all cricket knowledge.

Having enthused about day-night cricket, though, I have to say that what we currently have in this country is by no means the finished product. For a start, the quality of the portable floodlights is simply not up to scratch. So the side batting second is clearly at a disadvantage when dusk falls and the lights start to play their part. If we're going to take this business seriously, permanent floodlights are a must.

Secondly, the vast majority of the games are won by the side batting first. The lights are one factor, the English weather is another. Once the sun goes down, the dew starts to form and what was a flat, easy-paced pitch in the first innings can turn nasty with the ball seaming and nipping around all over the place.

One way around that problem would be to split the innings. We played the Lankies in a day-night friendly over at their place a couple of years ago and as an experiment, the innings were divided. They went in first for 20 overs and then we went out and had a bat. After the interval, they completed their innings under the lights and we rounded off the game with our second 20 overs. For my money, it worked well. Both sides had a taste of both sets of conditions. Mind you, we still lost.

And the elements will always be a potential problem in this country. Day-night cricket is essentially a game for balmy summer evenings when the adults can enjoy a picnic and a few beers or a glass of wine, when there's a play area for the little ones if they get bored and when people can sit around in shorts and a T-shirt without running the risk of contracting hypothermia. Unfortunately no one can guarantee the weather and it's not a bundle of fun for the fans if they are wrapped in blankets and for players if they have to wear three sweaters.

Even so, this kind of cricket is here to stay. I'm sure of that. I have played floodlit games at the Newlands Ground in Cape Town and watched day-night matches at the Melbourne Cricket Ground, and they must rank with Lord's as the finest cricket stadiums in the world. It was a marvellous experience. The sun goes down earlier in those parts of the world so the lights play a bigger part. They are so powerful that you might just as well be playing your cricket in the middle of a summer's afternoon. Conditions are dry, the weather is warm and it really is an incredible spectacle. The fans love it – just as they love it here. And when push comes to shove, this game is all about the fans, isn't it?

Yorkshire's day-night honeymoon is brief. They lose both games to Lancashire, who now occupy the position at the top of the National League table that Yorkshire occupied for so long at the start of the season. And far from pursuing silverware, Yorkshire are left anxiously looking over their shoulders as the clubs below them prepare to mount a late charge for safety. Both games against Lancashire end in near farce. At Headingley, it rains, the umpires appear to disagree over whether to continue and eventually the players leave the field with 28 balls left. At Old

Trafford, one of the floodlight pylon fails with Lancashire 19 runs short of a victory they eventually achieve after the scheduled finishing time. The lights are restored on their challenge; Yorkshire's hopes are left in the dark.

First lesson from Headingley's only day-night cricket of the summer: you can't see the rain coming in the dark. I was batting with Silvers at the death. We were chasing 150 and had reached 114 for 7 with 4.4 overs left. Not a straightforward task by any means. But we'd worked out that we'd see off their spinners, Watkinson and Muralitharan, and then give it a charge. You only need one big over in these situations and all of a sudden a steep target looks within range. But after two balls from Glenn Chapple's seventh over, down came the rain.

We had no idea it was on the way. Normally you see a big black cloud building up behind the football stand at Headingley and think hello, better get a move on here. But in the dark, it's fine one minute and pouring down the next. And when it comes to leaving the field, the rain always looks worse in the reflection of the lights.

Spoons and I wanted to stay on. OK, we didn't look like winning, but trudging off into the pavilion with 28 balls left is no way to finish a match like this in front of a near full house. Needless to say, the Lankies didn't agree. They were in the box seat. They knew that if we came off, our new target under the Duckworth-Lewis method would push the game out of our reach and they wasted no time in letting the umpires know the ball was getting wet, the outfield was slippy, conditions were impossible. Were they hell! It's just as bad for the batting side in the rain as the track starts to green up. But let's face it, we would have done exactly the same in their position.

With hindsight, we didn't really deserve to win. We bowled and fielded well enough to restrict them to 149 on a pitch that was never easy to bat on and we reckoned that if one player batted through, we would win the game. Michael Vaughan looked like doing just that but when he was out for 35 from 78 balls, we were already behind the rate. Once again, we performed without any real urgency, we allowed Ian

Austin to bowl nine overs for eight runs, we never built any partnerships and gradually fell away.

Back in the pit, it was all a bit desolate. We knew beforehand that we would have to beat Lancashire in both games to stay in with a shout of winning the National League and here we were, one down and one to play. A poor night.

And it was no better at Old Trafford five days later. A super spectacle, though. Lancashire have really set their stall out for the day-night stuff and there were over 10,000 people in the ground. And while the pitch once again prevented us from putting on a big-hitting, high-scoring spectacular, there was no shortage of controversy.

We batted unimpressively again and I found myself walking out to the middle in the 37th over with six wickets down and only 103 on the board. So to reach 153 wasn't a bad effort in the end. But it was well below par and once again I found myself unbeaten and unfulfilled.

Then Neil Harvey Fairbrother decided it was time to put the White Rose boys in their place once again. Harvey is a good lad but he's been a real thorn in our side down the years and he just set his stall out to be there at the end and win the game for Lancashire. And that's exactly what he did – aided and abetted by a floodlight failure which held up play for 17 minutes with Lancashire 19 short and 9.3 overs left. They would have got them, of course, and by the time the faulty pylon had been repaired their target was reduced by the Duckworth-Lewis method to just seven from 5.3 overs with five wickets standing. Not a formidable task.

David Byas was furious that Vera Duckworth should have been used after a floodlight failure but the umpires were, in fact, playing it by the book. The D-L method is principally for weather interruptions, though, and unless new regulations are introduced for power failures, it doesn't take a lot of imagination to foresee the day when someone, somewhere will pull a plug out to try and gain an advantage. Or am I just getting cynical in my old age?

So, another defeat. Relegation, we are warned, is a distinct possibility. I don't think so. We still have to play Kent at Canterbury, Leicestershire at Scarborough and Warwickshire at Headingley and I'm confident we'll pick up enough points to survive. Even so, it's hard to believe that seven weeks ago we were on top of the table with just one defeat from seven games. Now we've lost six in a row. We're in a rut, we're just not performing to our capabilities and it's very depressing.

CGU National League, Headingley. 12 August. Yorkshire Phoenix 114–7 lost to Lancashire Lightning 149 (C. Silverwood 3–22) by 14 runs (D-L method).

CGU National League, Old Trafford. 17 August. Yorkshire Phoenix (M.P. Vaughan 46) lost to Lancashire Lightning (N.H. Fairbrother 54*) by 5 wickets (D-L method).

GLOUCESTERSHIRE V YORKSHIRE, BRISTOL. NATWEST TROPHY SEMI-FINAL

Saturday, 7 August. The Yorkshire players make their way down to Bristol for what will be a make-or-break game against the side who lowered their colours in such emphatic style at Lord's a fortnight ago. Tomorrow's semi-final is going to be a tense old day for players and spectators alike, not to mention the umpires, David Constant and Roy Palmer, and their assistant, Chris Balderstone.

Umpires and umpiring have changed out of all recognition since I played my first game in the County Championship 14 years ago. In those days, the officials were very much part of the camaraderie of cricket. Players looked on them as friends and there was a tremendous rapport between the two sides. Even as a youngster, I was on first-name terms with most of them. A lot of the senior players had played with and against the umpires and would find time for a chat or a cup of tea before play and maybe a pint afterwards.

The umpires had a job to do, so did the players. And, while the current generation of cricketers making their mark at first-class level will hold their hands up in horror at this, we all did our best to help one another. First-class cricket has always been a tough arena, and rightly so. It is a professional sport after all. But hostilities were conducted in a far more civilised manner 15 years ago. I don't want to sound like an old fuddy duddy but I suppose the current approach to umpires is nothing more than a reflection of the way society in general has gone.

But enough of the homespun philosophy – although I do feel I am entitled to air my views on fair play after collecting an International Fair Play Award a few years ago. It happened against Leicestershire. James Whitaker nicked one, I took it on the half-volley, everyone went up, so did the umpire's finger and Whitaker started to walk . . . until I called him back. And he went on to get a ton. So much for honesty!

There was a time, though, when most batters would walk when they and everyone else within a 50-mile radius knew they had hit the ball. There was no point in making life difficult for the umpire who had a tough enough job to do anyway. Now, players never walk – and if the umpire gets it wrong, tough.

It's the same with dissent. I have always accepted an umpire's decision. Of course, it's no laughing matter when you are given out leg before when you know you have hit it; or if the finger goes up for a bat-pad and you never got an edge. But the decision has been made. And it has been made in good faith. So I simply cannot be doing with players who angrily slap their pad, nudge the bails off as they leave, abuse the umpire or return to the dressing-room and call him every name under the sun. He's just made a human error. He's doing a bloody hard job – and, in my view, doing it well.

I'll go further and disagree with most of my professional colleagues and claim that in my view, the standard of umpiring in the first-class game is good. The officials are fair and honest and while no one really stands out as being at the top of the tree, the overall standard is satisfactory. But it's a far more difficult job than it used to be.

Umpires, particularly at international level, work under intense pressure thanks to the all-seeing eye of television. At times I feel sorry for them. They are doing a hard job to the best of their ability and they end up getting pilloried for one minor error – thanks to the wonders of modern technology. The slow motion camera can just about identify the maker's name on the ball, enabling the experts to analyse every decision. Yet, looking at Channel Four's presentation of the Test series against New Zealand this summer, it's interesting to see just how often the umpires have been right after all. And they don't have the advantage of frame-by-frame replays when making most decisions.

That, inevitably, raises the question: why not? Technology has been used for some time now to enable the third umpire to pass judgement on line decisions like run-outs and stumpings and deciding whether the ball has crossed the boundary. Rightly so, too. It's an open and shut case; a player is either in or he's out. And far from creating an unnecessary distraction, the long wait for the red or green light to appear creates tension and atmosphere. So why not extend the use of technology?

This summer Channel Four has introduced the snickometer and the wicket-to-wicket shadow to help their pundits decide whether a batsman has got a touch or where the ball pitched in leg before appeals. As far as I can see, both these innovations work. So if the tele-experts can use them, why not the umpires as well?

The simple fact is that these days the officials are going to receive no help whatsoever from the players in reaching a decision. Indeed, cricketers will do everything in their power to influence a decision in their favour even if they know it is wrong. So let's give the umpires every tool at their disposal and take some of the chance out of those crucial leg before and bat-pad decisions.

In an ideal world, of course, technology would be available in every game, not just international cricket and the occasional big one-dayer. But I admit that the costs would be prohibitive. Even so there has to be a case for the third umpire being used in, for example, all four NatWest Trophy quarter-finals and not just the one game being televised. You can't have one set of rules for one match and another set for the other three.

As it happens our quarter-final at Old Trafford was televised and decisions were made with the help of the third umpire. Tomorrow at Bristol, David Constant and Roy Palmer will have the assistance of Chris Balderstone as the third official. And I, for one, will be heartily grateful for that.

Sunday, 8 August. The news from the battlefront is not good. Chris Silverwood, certain to be named in the England squad for Thursday's fourth Test against New Zealand at The Oval, will not play. His wife Emma has been injured in a road accident and he is staying at her bedside in hospital. Gavin Hamilton, another serious candidate for a place in the England line-up, will be missing, too. As is his wont, Hamilton was putting a brave face on his misfortunes when he arrived at Yorkshire's Bristol HQ last night. But as he joined his team-mates for breakfast, he was unusually subdued. Two hours later, a fitness test on his damaged right hamstring confirmed the obvious.

So Yorkshire take on Gloucestershire for the third time in four weeks without Silverwood, Hamilton, Darren Gough and Matthew Hoggard, a pace attack that would be the envy of virtually every other county. A sense of foreboding among the White Rose supporters who have travelled south is fuelled by the news that Mark Alleyne has won the toss and Gloucester will bat. As they did in the National League debacle at Cheltenham; as they did in the Super Cup final defeat at Lord's.

Anthony McGrath's late arrival for the Yorkshire team picture prompts much-needed laughter among the players and their followers and, from the vantage point of the Radio Leeds commentary post, it is apparent from the first few exploratory overs that on this occasion, Yorkshire are, in the current sporting vernacular, up for it. Today, Dr Jekyll is on duty for the White Rose, not Mr Hyde.

Paul Hutchison and Ryan Sidebottom bowl accurately and aggressively but without any fortune as Kim Barnett, in particular, and Tim Hancock ride their luck to post an opening partnership of 69. Barnett and Rob Cunliffe add a further 100 in 14 overs but the Yorkshire spinners, Ian Fisher and Michael Vaughan, bowl tightly and it is not until Sidebottom concedes 23 from a single over late in the innings that the wheels threaten to come off. Even so, a late flurry of wickets leaves Yorkshire chasing a target of 241 from their 50 overs on a pitch of variable pace and bounce. A tough assignment indeed.

The Radio Leeds summarisers, Worcestershire all-rounder Richard Illingworth and former Surrey and England batsman Graham Roope, agree without total conviction that Yorkshire can get the runs. Vaughan and Craig White are the men charged with giving them the solid start they have so often lacked and even though White is below par, they put on 37 for the first wicket.

With Vaughan completing a cultured half century and Byas and Richard Harden adding 85 in 18 overs, Yorkshire edge towards their target before the loss of Harden, Anthony McGrath and Bradley Parker in quick succession brings their progress to a shuddering halt. With two overs remaining, 32 are still needed. But Gary Fellows, a tiny Halifax all-rounder who rejoices in the nickname of Mouse, displays the heart of a lion as he clubs Mike Cawdron for 20 runs from the penultimate over.

The 100th over of the day is bowled, in an atmosphere of acute tension, by Ian Harvey, the hard-nosed Australian all-rounder who is, as Illingworth informs his listeners, the best 'death' bowler in the game. True to his reputation, he accounts for Fellows with his fourth delivery and as Blakey enters the fray at the fall of the sixth wicket, Yorkshire need eight runs from two balls to draw level and win the tie – having lost fewer wickets than the opposition.

Harvey's fifth ball is a waist-high full toss. Many an umpire would call it a no-ball in one-day cricket. Roy Palmer does not. Blakey's response is a cross-batted swing. He fails to connect properly, the batsmen cross for a single and Yorkshire have lost. 'Cricket can be a cruel game,' admits Byas afterwards. And how! Twice in the closing overs, the Yorkshire captain has been denied a certain four when the ball has ricocheted off the stumps at the opposite end of the wicket. Those eight runs would have won the match for his side.

Looking at the faces of the Yorkshire players as they leave the dressing-room and head for their cars, it is impossible not to feel sympathy. For the second time in three weeks they have been forced to endure the sight of the Gloucester players and their supporters frolicking on the pavilion balcony. At Lord's there were no excuses after a shoddy display. This time Yorkshire have glimpsed the promised land only to discover it is a mirage once again.

Vaughan, an unfailingly courteous man, walks unseeing past two reporters who are waiting in vain for an enlightening after-match quote. White and McGrath emerge from the dressing-room, their normal amiable demeanour replaced by blank, haunted stares. Words of sympathy from supporters of both sides go unheard. The captain's tie is awry as he appears briefly at the dressing-room door, anticipating questions from the media. To his evident relief, the reporters have not yet arrived. He will later offer the view that Yorkshire can take a lot of encouragement out of the match. They have not buckled in any department and, ultimately, have come very close indeed. Fisher and Fellows have put down markers for the future. He is proud of his team. He can also be proud of his own performance.

But in the subdued light of the corridor, as the Gloucester party gets under way in earnest, his wicketkeeper and senior professional appears to have aged ten years. Blakey's face is gaunt and pale, disappointment etched in every line. Let anyone who criticises this man for 'not being bothered' about Yorkshire cricket take a look at him now. Words of consolation are meaningless and superfluous. 'Six runs,' he laments. 'Six runs! It might as well be 600.' It is going to be a long journey home.

NatWest Trophy semi-final, Bristol. 15 August. Yorkshire 234–6 (D. Byas 71*, M.P. Vaughan 54) lost to Gloucestershire 240–7 (K.J. Barnett 98) by 6 runs.

LANCASHIRE V YORKSHIRE, OLD TRAFFORD

Thursday, 19 August. The Battle of the Roses. There was a time when this was the most significant match on the Championship calendar. In a bygone era, immortalised in the writing of Sir Neville Cardus, the captain of the batting side would send his opening batsmen out to do battle in front of a packed house on the first morning with the strict instruction: 'No fours before lunch.' Avoiding defeat was everything in these tribal wars of attrition between the great northern rivals. Today, battle is joined in front of a small gathering, most of whom are more aware of the historical significance of the match than many of the players. Blakey is one of a select band of Yorkshire batsmen to score a century on his Roses début – in 1987, at Old Trafford of all places! The last of his nine Championship centuries was against the same opponents at Headingley in 1996.

One way or another it was quite a way to embark on my Roses career. As a kid I was brought up on heroic tales of Roses cricket and back in the '70s and early '80s the matches used to be televised live. I always made a point of watching . . . and dreaming that one day I would actually play against Yorkshire's historic rivals. So you can imagine what a big day it was when my chance came at Old Trafford on 13 June 1987. And what a dramatic match it was.

After a series of declarations, we were set 287 to win in 65 minutes plus 20 overs. I was called into the action in the second over of the innings when Ashley Metcalfe was dismissed for nought. Martyn Moxon and I put on 80 for the second wicket but after eight wickets fell for 101, we were struggling at 223 for 9 with 17.5 overs left. I was joined by our last man, Stuart Fletcher.

Now Fletch was a more than useful seam bowler but, by his own admission, not a batsman to strike terror into the opposition ranks . . . a walking bonus point, as we would say. And the Lankies clearly fancied their chances of mopping up what was left of our resistance. They reckoned without two players who had grown up together as rivals in the Huddersfield League.

Fletch dug in and soon after his arrival, I reached my first Roses century. I wish I could recall my exact emotions but while I was thrilled to bits to make a hundred against the old enemy, we still had a match to save.

As we crept ever nearer to safety, Lancashire's efforts started to grow more and more frantic. And the tension was heightened when Fletch was given not out to a bat-pad chance. I was 22 yards away at the other end and had almost exactly the same view as the umpire – and there was no way I would have given it. But the whole Lancashire close cordon had gone up, and that's usually a pretty ominous sign. Fletch looked a bit sheepish when we met for our mid-wicket confab between the overs and if the atmosphere had been hot before the incident, it was positively explosive afterwards.

The Lancashire players have never been backward in coming forward with the sledging and no one was more vociferous than Paul Allott. Walt, as he is known throughout the game, is a good guy and has done well in the broadcasting world since he retired. But he certainly wouldn't want his remarks that day repeated on air.

Not that it worried Fletch and me. We survived and left Lancashire claiming that the Fletcher incident would cost them the County Championship. It probably did – because they finished just four points behind the winners, Nottinghamshire. Jack Simmons went as far as to accuse Stuart of cheating, remarks that were widely reported in the national press the following morning. Jack collected a hefty fine for his trouble.

But the battle obviously gave me a taste for Roses warfare because in the return match at Headingley, I made an unbeaten 79 in our first innings to take my Roses tally for that year to 207 without having my colours lowered. I collected my first Roses duck the following season. But in all honesty, as far as the players of both sides are concerned, the Roses match is just another game these days.

It's a different matter when there's a spot of one-day glory at stake in front of a full house at either Headingley or Old Trafford and over the years, we've had some classic encounters. Those games are charged with an electric atmosphere that I have never found elsewhere. But in the Championship, any extra rivalry is generated among the supporters and the players approach the match with the same attitude as any other fixture. It's good to win, of course, not least because it gives our fans a tremendous kick. But then again, it's good to win any game, any time, anywhere, against any opposition.

And I'm sorry if this sounds like heresy but the Yorkshire players probably get on better with their Lancashire counterparts than with any other team in the Championship. We're northern lads, we're peas from the same pod. A lot of us have played against one another in inter-county matches right from our schoolboy days and on through age group games to the Second XI and finally the first-class arena. I have played representative cricket with several Lancashire players down the years and I've been on England A and full tours with Mike Atherton and Neil Fairbrother and an A tour with Warren Hegg. And I have a tremendous amount of respect for Lancashire as a team, particularly in one-day cricket over the last ten years or so.

Having said that, it will give me and the rest of the Yorkshire side the greatest of pleasure if we give them a good hiding in their own backyard over the next four days. It will finally enable us to make up for the victory that got away two years ago.

That was a game we dominated right from the start and at the end of the third day, we were 318 in front with five wickets in hand, planning to make quick runs for an hour or so the following morning and then bowl out the Lankies on what was a rapidly deteriorating pitch. Or that was the plan, anyway.

We went to bed on the Friday night, confident of scoring a victory that would maintain our Championship challenge. I was vaguely conscious of a heavy downpour at some stage of the night but we awoke to a bright, sunny August morning and after breakfast, set off for Old Trafford. I reached the ground just at around 9.30 a.m. to be informed by the car park attendant that the game was off. Assuming this was a lame attempt at Lancashire humour, I gave him a friendly smile and proceeded to the dressing-room. As I reached the pavilion entrance, I was given the same piece of information by another member of the Lancashire staff.

Sure enough, the shell-shocked atmosphere in our dressing-room confirmed my growing fears. The square was fine. But on the actual pitch there was an area at one end from where the stumps would be pitched to about eight feet down the track that had turned to mud after overnight rain had leaked through the covers. No one would be playing cricket on that.

To this day, everyone at Lancashire will swear until they're blue in the face that it was an accident. But Old Trafford is a Test match venue, remember, not a little outground in the sticks. And accidents of that magnitude aren't supposed to happen. It was all very suspicious and you could have cut the atmosphere with a knife as the Lancashire officials tried to explain what had happened to David Byas. I don't think I've ever seen him so angry.

In the final analysis, though, there we were, standing under blue skies looking at a mudbath that should have been a cricket pitch. There was no point crying over spilt milk. The only option was to hump the gear into the car and drive back across the Pennines.

I ended up going to The McAlpine Stadium to watch Huddersfield Town play Sheffield United. Needless to say, people kept coming up to ask what we'd won by. They couldn't believe it when I told them the match had been abandoned. So Roses rivalry or not, there will be a bit of two-year-old needle in the air over the next four days. And who knows what kind of pitch might lie in store for us this time.

Four days? Make that two and a bit. Or, to be precise, just seven sessions. That's how long it takes Lancashire to cruise to a ten-wicket victory after dismissing Yorkshire for a paltry 67 after rain delayed the start until after lunch on the first day. Michael Vaughan, clearly aware of age-old Roses traditions, set a new Yorkshire Roses record by batting for 59 minutes and 47 balls before getting off the mark. And Blakey, who joined Vaughan with Yorkshire on 26 for 6, finished with his side's highest score – 19. Lancashire duly eased their way to their fifth successive Roses win and, apart from the battle to stay in the First Division of the National League and qualify for the top division of next season's County Championship, Yorkshire's season is effectively over.

It's a sickening feeling, deep down in the pit of my stomach. On the morning of Sunday, 1 August, Yorkshire Day, we stood on the threshold of a glorious season. We were about to start the Super Cup final at Lord's, we had reached the semi-final of the NatWest Trophy, we were second in the National League. And above all, we were very much in contention for the County Championship.

Now, after a depressing series of defeats, I am left to face the grim reality that once again Yorkshire are not going to win any silverware. I can't really take it in, to be honest. I just cannot understand what's gone so horribly wrong; why we have under-achieved once again. Are we good enough? I have always maintained that we are. But you can't argue with results. And right now, hanging on to qualify for the first division of the County Championship next season and surviving in the top division of the National League are the priorities. We can forget any talk of trophies for another year. Recriminations have already begun among supporters.

God knows we've worked hard enough, though. We put in hours of training and practice pre-season and everyone gave 110 per cent on the tour to South Africa. We've followed the expert advice on what to eat, when to rest, how to train and on mental preparation. We've given it everything in the nets and spent hours practising match situations out in the middle. In short, we've done all the groundwork.

But after starting well enough and building the platform for real success, our whole world has fallen apart in less than a month. I have every sympathy for the people out there who pay their money to watch and support us. But if only they knew how distressing this situation is for me. I am devastated. I've had all sorts of people ringing me up, asking where we've gone wrong and I've tried to put a brave face on it, but it hasn't been easy.

Of course the players will keep pulling together to turn things round. We'll net before we play at Nottingham on Tuesday and who knows, we might go right through to the end of the season without another defeat. On ability alone, we're more than capable of that.

But it's too late, I'm afraid. Our season has caved in. It's disheartening for us and, of course, for the spectators. I can understand their frustrations. And already there are letters to the local papers calling for heads to roll. This stage of the season is a dangerous time for Yorkshire cricketers – just ask Peter Hartley and one or two more down the years who have suddenly had the rug pulled from under their feet. But I intend to be around for a while yet. I have a year left on my contract and all I want to do is carry on playing cricket for Yorkshire for as long as I possibly can.

Yorkshire cricket has been my life since I joined the staff 16 years ago and I don't intend to throw it away now. But when the season ends I will take time out to look at my own performance. I have already explained how tough it is to be batting down at number eight or nine and how I don't feel I can make the contribution I know I am capable of. So I'll have a chat with David and Martyn, see how they assess things and take it from there. In an ideal world, I would bat higher up the order. But I can understand their reluctance to promote me if it means a younger player missing out. I just want to do myself justice. And it isn't easy at the moment, believe me.

Looking back at the Roses match débâcle, though, I might not be saying all this if the coin had fallen the other way round. For everything hinged on the toss. We looked at the wicket in advance and said, 'Right, if we win the toss, we'll have a bat. It's going to crack up and spin later on.' It did. But by then the game was over. Yes, we won the toss and, just as Lancashire would have chosen to do, we batted. But no one in the world could have predicted how the wicket would play. I firmly believe batting on that pitch was virtually impossible.

It was a bit wet after the two-hour delay. The ball swung and seamed and every time it pitched, it left a little indentation. They bowled in the right areas and it jagged around all over the place. Michael Vaughan looked in reasonable nick but it still took him an hour to get off the mark. Four of our first seven batsmen were out first ball and not even the sternest critic of our batting line-up could claim that is a normal course of events.

I joined Virgil at 26 for 6 and if I had not survived a reasonably straightforward chance in the slips on one, we could have been all out for less than 30. As it was, we managed to put a bit of a stand together and Yorkshire reached the dizzy heights of 67 all out. However positive you try to be, there's no way back from there.

If we had bowled first, I'm sure it would have been a similar story and, of course, the captain has come in for his share of criticism for choosing to bat. With the magical gift of hindsight, it was the wrong decision. But, like I say, Lancashire would have batted first, too, because they could not have forecast how the pitch would have behaved any more than we could.

Even so, our performance in the field also left a lot to be desired. Andrew Flintoff hammered the ball to all parts for a thunderous 160 after we thought I had caught him for just 18. The umpire didn't; end of story. We dropped five catches as they compiled 314 and, for the third time this season, just managed to avoid an innings defeat.

So all in all, August has been a wicked month for Yorkshire cricket. And, for better or worse, it isn't over yet.

PPP Healthcare County Championship, Old Trafford. 19–22 August. Yorkshire 67 and 277 (D. Byas 66) lost to Lancashire 314 (A. Flintoff 160) and 34–0 by 10 wickets.

NOTTINGHAMSHIRE V YORKSHIRE, TRENT BRIDGE

Tuesday, 24 August. Like most professional clubs in a wide variety of sports, Yorkshire employ a sports psychologist. And after their recent travails, it's fair to say his services are likely to be in demand as the players prepare for the Championship game at Trent Bridge. It is a match Yorkshire dare not lose if they want to avoid an undignified scramble for a place in next season's First Division.

We need to be positive. But that's not easy when in the space of three weeks you've lost a Lord's final, a NatWest semi-final and seen your dreams of two championships go down the pan. Hopefully, though, the time we have put in with our sports psychologist will lift us. He is Malcolm Cook, a Scot who has worked with several football teams, including Liverpool, and on a one-to-one basis with a lot of top sportsmen.

He came to Yorkshire after meeting up with Martyn Moxon on one of the ECB winter management courses and he's been with us off and on for the last couple of years. But not on a regular basis by any means. And we found that the effect of our sessions tended to wear off before he came back for another stint.

We all like the guy and his approach to the job so we asked if it would be possible for him to come in regularly during the season. He arrived when we reported back for pre-season training and while he isn't employed by the club full-time, he's been around a lot.

It's easy for people to scoff at the idea of sports psychology but it's something I take seriously. It's about positive thinking, team bonding, belief in your own individual ability and the ability of the team, working as a unit. We're all good players – if we weren't we wouldn't be first-class cricketers. But the crucial difference between winners and losers can so often be in the mind. If you genuinely believe you are better than your opponents, you are nine-tenths of the way there and the odds are you will perform well.

But for one reason or another, possibly because we have a lot of young lads in the side, we've been a little bit timid in our approach over the last couple of seasons. We haven't really believed, deep down, that we were going to go out there and win. We haven't backed ourselves as individuals.

They were the kind of things we wanted to eliminate when we first sat down with Malcolm. He asked us to identify one specific area where we had fallen down and virtually everyone came up with the same answer: lack of killer instinct. Too often we've had teams on the rack and not polished them off.

Malcolm believes that inhibitions play a big part in a team under-achieving and says that we have to be completely honest with one another if we are to function efficiently as a unit. So he encouraged us to analyse one another's performance and contribution over the last couple of seasons, no punches pulled.

Now that isn't as easy as it sounds. It's one thing to think in your own mind that one of your team-mates has been under-performing . . . but a very different thing to tell him so to his face in front of 20 other people. It would be the same in any walk of life. So understandably there was a fair amount of reticence to begin with. But Malcolm has kept pressing the point and we've become far more open as the season has developed.

It showed up well in that team meeting we had before the NatWest win over Lancashire at Old Trafford. As I said at the time, there was some really straight talking in there – but no grudges held afterwards. And the following day we turned in arguably our best performance of the season so far.

In another effort to coax the inhibitions out of the squad he asked us to write down an individual assessment of all the other players as a person and as a cricketer – good or bad. Thankfully, nobody took a real pop at me, even if some of the younger lads do keep calling me a bandy-legged old so-and-so. My batting technique came under scrutiny and I was also described as experienced – in other words, old. But it was nice to hear that generally speaking, the lads reckoned I was a good man in a crisis.

We also have individual cards from Malcolm setting out our strengths and weaknesses. Each player has a nickname. I am Richard the Lionheart. Not bad, eh? Certainly better than Richard the Third or Dick Head, as I have been known in the past. Or, for that matter, Racing Dog. That was my first nickname back in the mid '80s and I was quite flattered. I assumed it referred to my speed between the wickets and agility in the field. It was a while before I discovered it was a reference to my personal anatomy!

But enough of that. I have no doubt that after working with Malcolm we are far more honest with one another and probably a better unit for that. But the bottom line, of course, is that we haven't won anything. And we aren't going to win anything this season. So that will provide ammunition to the critics of sports psychology who claim it is a load of mumbo jumbo. I don't accept that at all. And I believe that in time, our work with Malcolm will bear fruit.

Like it or not, times have changed from the days when sportsmen went through a few basic training routines and turned up on match day to do the business out in the middle. Nowadays there are sports psychologists, nutritionists, personal trainers and all sorts of other people to advise us about what we eat, how we should rest, how we should train, how we should prepare, what our mental approach should be, how we should handle the media. And I'm not just talking about cricket. These people are involved right across the sporting spectrum.

And surely it would be a case of gross negligence if we ignored them? OK, we haven't won anything in 1999 but by taking on board every modern technique available to us, we have given ourselves the best chance of doing so.

From a purely personal point of view, I have enjoyed working with Malcolm. He's a good man, the kind of guy who can find something upbeat and positive in every situation. I'm still pretty low right now . . . but if Malcolm walked into the room, he'd cheer me up, get me thinking more positively. And a lot of what he has told us about our approach to sport can be taken into what might be called the real world, too.

Sports psychology or not, Yorkshire respond to their drubbing at Old Trafford in the best possible way. In a low-scoring match on what might be politely termed a sporting pitch, Nottinghamshire are beaten by three wickets with a day to spare. And after scoring a half century in the first innings and sharing a decisive partnership with Hamilton in the second, Blakey can be pleased with his contribution. So, too, can Silverwood, who clubbed 25 off 14 deliveries to clinch victory. But for the second successive game, the quality of the playing surface raises serious questions.

Quite frankly, and forgive me for putting it so bluntly, the majority of the pitches we have played on this season have been absolute shite. OK, as a team we haven't batted well and our return of just 17 batting points to date, only Worcestershire have picked up fewer, tells its own story. But there have been only three pitches all year when batting has not been bloody hard work.

We had a good one for the game against Somerset at Taunton which yielded 987 runs and a definite result, unfortunately not in our favour. Then we came across a belter against Essex at Chelmsford and what happened? Virgil and Stuart Law both scored a hundred in each innings and the match went into the final session before we won by 74 runs. A good game of cricket for everyone involved. And finally at Scarborough last month, we expected a seamer but it turned out to be a good cricket track which almost produced a result.

But generally, both at home and on our travels, we have been plagued by uneven bounce and exaggerated seam movement. People like Blewett, Vaughan and Wood are good batsmen, no question, but they have struggled all season to give us a decent start. It's certainly opened Dick Harden's eyes. Down the years at Taunton as a Somerset player, he's scored heavily and no one would deny that he's a good player. But now he's come to Yorkshire he's found out the hard way how difficult it is to make your living as a batsman up here.

Every batsman's confidence has taken a battering and even when they do get on a decent surface they aren't moving their feet properly or looking to be aggressive; sure signs that confidence is at a low ebb. But the problem doesn't just exist on White Rose territory. All over the circuit, players are going into a match thinking about how they will survive instead of where they will look to score off each bowler. They are thinking that sooner or later there's an unplayable ball waiting for them.

Some of the Notts boys were telling me that they have been playing on these kind of surfaces all season. Clive Rice, their coach, believes he can back his seam attack against anyone else and wants green pitches. So here we are at the end of August and not a single Championship game has gone into the fourth day at Trent Bridge. That's an incredible statistic.

Tim Robinson, a good enough player to score over 1500 Test runs and not far short of 30,000 in his career, has had enough. He scored nought and six in this game and still managed to be hit on the hands several times. I batted longer than anybody else and I'm black and blue all over, chest, forearm, side of the leg. I never felt in and I frequently played and missed. It was a case of riding the blows, keeping out the straight ones and having a dip if something came along with a bit of width.

All the seamers picked up wickets but, quite honestly, I would have fancied my chances on that track. I would eventually have put one in the right place and either the batsman would have got an edge or he would have been trapped leg before.

The trouble is that results are paramount, particularly with places in the top division next season at stake. But until we do something about improving the pitches we play on, we can forget about producing a successful England side. As I've said before, we need surfaces where batsmen can play a long innings and where bowlers have to work hard for their wickets.

So whatever happened to the ECB directive that pitches should be straw-coloured and have pace and bounce? I suspect that even if counties prepared pitches that looked OK, they would find a way of making sure there was still plenty of movement. But behind the pitch directive there is back-up legislation in place to penalise counties for poor surfaces.

But what happens when they don't comply? A pitch inspector is despatched to take a look, he files a report, the county is slapped on the wrist and told not to be naughty – and then carries on doing exactly the same thing.

And if one county is going to prepare so-called result pitches to suit their bowlers, then so is just about everyone else in order to keep up. They would be crazy not to. We head off to Scarborough next week for an important four-day game against Kent. Until recently, the North Marine Road pitches were always excellent batting surfaces and no doubt we could produce another shirt front this time. But how would we feel if, as our match petered out into a draw on the final day, our main rivals for a place in the top three were taking a day off after finishing early on a result strip?

I can state quite categorically that pitches have deteriorated massively in recent years. It's not that long ago that if you lost the toss you could resign yourself to being out in the field all day and facing a total of over 300. In 1999, teams are being bowled out for less than 100 on a fairly regular basis and the fielding side can expect to be batting after tea. Take a look at the teletext on the first day of a so-called four-day game and all over the place there are scores like 47 for 7 or 63 for 6.

And the Test grounds are just as bad as the average county surfaces. In our Championship game against Warwickshire at Edgbaston the ball was taking off from a length and flying over my shoulder, or keeping low – a very poor surface.

So as the debate continues to rage over England's poor batting performance in the series defeat by New Zealand this summer, just remember that it isn't all down to poor technique. And I repeat: how can we possibly produce Test batsmen and bowlers on these pitches?

PPP Healthcare County Championship, Trent Bridge. 24–27 August. Yorkshire 185 (R.J. Blakey 60) and 144–7 (G.M. Hamilton 43*) beat Nottinghamshire 184 (Hamilton 5–30, C. White 4–44) and 144 (White 4–32) by 3 wickets.

KENT SPITFIRES V YORKSHIRE PHOENIX, CANTERBURY. NATIONAL LEAGUE

Saturday, 28 August. It could have been the NatWest Trophy final against Somerset at Lord's. Instead, Yorkshire face a Bank Holiday trip to Canterbury for tomorrow's National League game against Kent. With the England selectors due to name their party for the winter tour to South Africa on Monday, the long drive offers a chance to reflect on England tours past.

My England career began and ended in tears. They were tears of joy and pride when I walked out with my England team-mates to make my début in a Texaco Trophy match against Pakistan at Lord's on 22 August 1992. And tears of despair as, seven months later, I sat alone and dejected in a hotel room in Bombay after scoring just seven runs in four Test innings against India. I played in a couple of one-day internationals at the end of that 1992–93 tour of the sub-continent but when I returned home, I knew I hadn't done myself justice.

But even though my days as a full England player were short and not particularly sweet, I have no regrets. It is every cricketer's dream to represent his country and I have done so. Of course I wanted to play more Tests and more one-day internationals but look at the record books and you will see the name of R.J. Blakey among the list of England players. No one will ever be able to take that away from me.

I first arrived on the international scene as an England Under-19 player in 1984 and my first tour was an Under-19 expedition to the

West Indies in 1984–85. While some of my team-mates like Phil DeFreitas, Mike Roseberry, David Ripley and Phil Tufnell are still playing county cricket, the others have fallen by the wayside for one reason or another.

It was a good tour, though, and a steep learning curve in the art of playing fast bowling. Every side we faced seemed to have a budding Marshall, Holding or Garner in their line-up and there were a few decent batters around, too – men like Carl Hooper, Jimmy Adams and Roland Holder.

My first room-mate? The Cat, Phil Tufnell, a man destined to play a significant role in my England career a few years down the road. I was a clean-living lad at the time and took myself off to bed at around 9 p.m. to be ready for the battles ahead the following day. It will not surprise you to learn that The Cat did not share my philosophy and used to come blundering into the room rather later than that. His lifestyle didn't seem to affect his bowling, though, so perhaps he had the right idea after all.

Tuffers was not involved in my next two England adventures, the 1989–90 A team tour to Kenya and Zimbabwe and the trip to Pakistan and Sri Lanka the following year. I enjoyed them tremendously – for both the cricket, the travel and the comradeship. The captains, Mark Nicholas and Hugh Morris, did an excellent job on and off the field and the spirit on both tours was first-class.

County cricket is a funny old life. You play against people year in and year out without ever really knowing what they're like. After opposing someone over 22 yards of cricket pitch it's quite easy to form a wrong impression and decide he is a total prat. And it's only when you're thrown into a touring situation with the same guy that he turns out to be good bloke after all. You learn what makes him tick on and off the field.

With Andy Afford, the former Notts player who was a room-mate in Zimbabwe, the answer was tea. I've never known anyone consume so much in a single day. He had the kettle on before breakfast, downed a few cups with his meal and then as soon as he got back into the room, the kettle was on again. Incredible.

Camaraderie or not, though, that first tour started disastrously. We warmed up for the Zimbabwe leg of the trip with ten days in Kenya, based at a magnificent old colonial pile. Robin Boyd-Moss, the

Northants player, was coaching over there during the winter and he recommended us to try a Chinese restaurant in downtown Nairobi. When in Kenya, do as the English do, I suppose. So we all set off for a team meal and a good night. And it was – until I woke up at around 3 a.m. feeling distinctly unwell.

I was violently sick and decided the best course of action was to go along to our physio Dave Roberts's room and see if he had anything that might cure the problem. I was fifth in the queue. And by the time morning broke, ten players had gone down with salmonella poisoning. Steve Rhodes, the Worcestershire wicketkeeper, spent a night in hospital. It was so bad that we had to call off our one-day game against a Kenya Cricket Association Chairman's XI because we couldn't field a side.

But once we got to Zimbabwe and started in earnest, things could hardly have gone better for me. As luck would have it, I had arranged to spend the close season playing in Zimbabwe, so when I was chosen for the tour party, I decided to spend the first three months of the winter there anyway. In that time, I became thoroughly at home with the conditions and faced most of the players I subsequently came up against with England.

I also made a stack of runs and carried that form into the tour games. In the three first-class matches we played I made 337 runs at an average of 84.25, including a career-best 221 in the second unofficial Test in Bulawayo. In that game I shared a third-wicket partnership of 157 with another promising young player by the name of Mike Atherton.

Even at that stage, Athers was carrying the label of FEC, or Future England Captain. Or that's the polite, official version anyway. I got to know Athers quite well. He has always given the impression of being the kind of man who doesn't smile too much – hence his Captain Grumpy nickname a few years later when he finally made it to the top job. But nothing could be further from the truth. Mike has a smashing dry sense of humour and was always ready to play a leading role in the dressing-room banter.

There was plenty of that on a happy tour all round and my career-best score had the critics raving about me. I was labelled an England batting star of the future. But even then I was aware that the wheel always turns full circle and one day those same critics would be having a go at me instead. Sure enough, that happened in India three years later. But that's another story.

I returned from Zimbabwe with my reputation enhanced and when the 1990 edition of *Wisden* was published the tour report stated that 'Blakey showed the temperament and remorseless concentration required for five-day cricket.' All good stuff.

Twelve months later I was off on my travels again, this time embarking at Heathrow for an eight-week tour of Pakistan and Sri Lanka. Or that was the plan. But we hadn't been in Pakistan for many minutes before the Gulf War erupted. Pakistan was a highly volatile environment and we were confined to our hotel in Lahore, protected by armed guards. It was a scary time, particular for the older players with wives and kids back home.

In the end, the powers-that-be decided it was time to jump ship, Sri Lanka offered us a revised tour itinerary of six weeks and off we went. It was another good tour with a great bunch of lads. Marvellous beaches, nights out in Colombo riding around on rickshaws . . . happy times.

But the humidity! Down the years, I have often tried to describe the conditions out there to friends, only to be accused of exaggeration. But no. I have never played in heat like it. One lap around the ground before the start of play and it was time to take water on board. The sweat just poured out of me all day. Here, when it's particularly hot, we have a mid-session drinks break; in Sri Lanka, the regulations state there must be two per session. You have to re-hydrate constantly – and even then some players struggled. Tim Munton of Warwickshire had to leave the field one day when he started having hallucinations because he was so dehydrated. And we were all affected to a lesser degree.

Still, it was all good experience and a vital part of the learning process. On a purely individual note, I didn't perform as well as I had the previous year but, according to most pundits, I returned home with my reputation intact. And six months later, I was pulling on an England sweater for the first time.

The 1992 season was a good one for me. I topped the 1,000 run mark for Yorkshire, averaging 46.30, and as the summer progressed there were whispers that I wasn't a million miles away from an England call. It came one morning when I was at home on my own. The phone rang, it was Mickey Stewart, then the England manager. 'We'd like you to come down to Lord's as part of the Texaco Trophy squad.' My heart missed a beat. 'You'll probably only get one game – and you might not even manage that. But we want you to be there.'

I put the phone down and for about five minutes I ran around the house, waving my arms about and shouting 'Yes, Yes, Yes' at the top of my voice. I dread to think what the neighbours thought. It took me a while before it started to really sink in. But the following morning there was my name in the papers as a member of the England squad for a three-match Texaco Trophy series against Pakistan. I linked up with the rest of the lads in London, went through the training sessions and the press photocalls. There were some huge names in the squad which consisted of Gooch, Stewart, Robin Smith, Fairbrother, Lamb, Hick, Botham, Reeve, Lewis, DeFreitas, Illingworth – and Blakey.

And I was made to feel part of the set-up from the start. There was no hint in those days of new players not being made to feel welcome in an England dressing-room. People like Both and Lamby went out of their way to make me feel at home. It was quite moving, really. Then, after missing the first game at Trent Bridge, I was picked for the second match. At Lord's of all places.

Graham Gooch should have been skipper but cried off on the morning of the game. Alec Stewart took over and it was felt at the time that he couldn't handle the triple responsibility of captain, opening batsman and wicketkeeper. Sounds familiar? So 25 minutes before the game was due to start, Goochie came along and said, 'Dick, you're playing.' This time the heart missed a couple of beats. But I have to confess that once I had got the kit on, I sneaked away, found a mirror and just looked at myself wearing an England strip.

There can be no better place to play your first game for England than Lord's and as I walked through the Long Room there were all the old buffers in their bacon and egg ties, no doubt thinking, 'Who's that chap?' They applauded us down the steps and out on to the pitch. I remember having a good look around and thinking, 'It doesn't get much better than this.' And yes, there were a few tears as I made my way towards the middle.

Chris Lewis bowled the first over to Aamir Sohail and just before the umpire called play I looked to my left. There in the slips were Ian Botham and Allan Lamb, two of the game's legends. I knew then that

I had finally made it. I remember thinking, 'No matter what happens in the rest of my career, I have stood here at Lord's as an England player.' OK, I haven't appeared in as many games as I would have liked but I have still played for my country at the headquarters of cricket and stood alongside two of the game's biggest names.

I enjoyed the whole experience. I can't remember a lot about the game except that we lost and I made 25 before I was bowled by Waqar Younis. I kept wicket OK, too, but generally the whole shooting match went by in a bit of a blur.

Inevitably, after winning a place in the end-of-season Texaco series, there were plenty of rumours that I was in the frame for the winter tour to India. But I tried to take those with a pinch of salt until any official announcement was made. Back in 1992, I still enjoyed a lie-in and I was in bed when the phone rang mid-morning. It was my dad. He'd seen on the teletext that I'd been picked for the winter tour. The news was still sinking in when all hell broke loose. Reporters on the phone, Yorkshire asking me to go to Headingley for a Press call, local television and radio wanting interviews. My feet hardly touched the ground for 24 hours. Little did I realise in my excitement that I had been selected for what has subsequently gone down on record as the Tour from Hell.

It wasn't that bad, of course. And there will always be some happy memories of my passage to India amid the nightmares. But overall, it was three months on the rack and the flak started flying within minutes of the squad being announced. These were the players who made the trip: Gooch (capt.), Stewart (vice-capt.), Atherton, Blakey, DeFreitas, Emburey, Fairbrother, Gatting, Hick, Jarvis, Lewis, Malcolm, Reeve, Smith, Taylor, Tufnell. And straight away the critics pounced on the absence of two players, David Gower and Jack Russell.

Gower, they argued, was not just one of the all-time batting greats. Even at 35, he was still the best player of spin in the country and England would need all his skill in that department against the Indians. And, of more significance to me, the choice of Alec Stewart and myself ahead of an out-and-out specialist wicketkeeper like Russell was also pilloried. Now Jack Russell has no greater admirer than me. He was and, in my view, still is the best wicketkeeper around. But I felt I was entitled to a fair crack of the whip – at least before a ball was bowled. And while a cross-section of the Press comments were favourable, some of the so-called eminent correspondents from the quality newspapers wrote in no uncertain terms that the selection of Blakey was disastrous.

So was the tour. We were the first England team ever to lose every match in a Test series in India. And to make matters worse we lost to Sri Lanka as well and fared poorly in the one-dayers, losing five out of eight against the two opposing countries.

My contribution was negligible. I played in two Tests, in Madras and Bombay. And while overall I was happy with my wicketkeeping, I failed to come to terms with the Indian spinners Kumble and Raju (I wasn't alone in that, either) and managed just seven runs in four innings. I wouldn't attempt to make excuses for that performance but no one in their right mind would suggest I went into those two Test matches with any proper preparation under my belt.

I had arrived in India just after Christmas feeling pretty confident, particularly about my batting after my good year with Yorkshire. I was less comfortable about the wicketkeeping as I had only been doing the job full-time since 1991. I was still feeling under pressure at Yorkshire and even though I had worked with Alan Knott in the build-up to the tour, I was nothing like as happy in the job as I am today. Even so, when the first game was played on 3 January, I was upbeat about my prospects. I accepted that I was basically out there as an understudy in both capacities but reckoned I could do enough to climb another rung up the international ladder. Instead I fell off and hit the deck with a bump.

I didn't get out into the middle until we played the Rest of India at Vishakapatnam on 5 February, the seventh game of the tour. A bitter disappointment. I tried to stay positive about the situation, to keep my spirits up and do everything that was expected of me as a tourist. But, with the best will in the world, five weeks of nets and carrying drinks is not easy. And no one will need reminding that conditions off the field in India are a million miles away from anything we are used to back home.

When I finally made my first appearance, I did OK with the bat, making 63 not out. But the game will always be remembered for the incidents that followed my missed stumping off Phil Tufnell, my room-mate in the West Indies on that Under-19 tour. Sachin Tendulkar was batting, I was behind the stumps and The Cat was in the middle of a pretty average spell. He had been no-balled eleven times for over-stepping and was not a happy bunny. Eventually, Phil found the perfect delivery, Sachin went down the track, got an inside edge and presented me with a clear stumping chance. Instead the ball hit the edge of my glove and the opportunity was lost.

The Cat showed his disapproval in no uncertain terms, turning the air blue as he snatched his cap from the umpire before kicking it along the ground in a fit of anger. He stalked off to his fielding station after exchanging more angry words with his team-mates. On a tour when his behaviour was under official scrutiny, he found himself the subject of banner headlines the next day and was fined five hundred pounds by the tour management. He responded by taking four wickets in 5.3 overs as the opposition lost five wickets for just eleven runs.

I have never believed that his outburst was against me personally, although that was a view widely held at the time, particularly in the papers. His frustrations just got the better of him and he boiled over in truly spectacular style. But the tantrum was aimed at the world in general and not specifically directed at me. Needless to say, I was just as down about missing the chance as he was. Afterwards he went to his corner of the dressing-room and I went to mine and we got on with the rest of our lives. Nothing more was said about it between us, although I was inundated with calls from people back home asking what had gone on. So it was a big story, although to me it had been blown out of all proportion.

But let me say for the record that any suggestions of a rift between me and The Cat are way off the mark. I have always reckoned Phil is a pretty good guy and there are no problems between us. We usually take time out to have a chat when Yorkshire play Middlesex and the events at Vishakapatnam have been water under the bridge for a long time now.

Five days after the rumpus, we were both back on duty again. This time for England in the second Test at Madras. And I had a plate of prawns to thank for my first England cap. Gooch, Gatting and one or two of the team had eaten in the hotel's Chinese restaurant the previous night; on the face of it, a reasonable idea. It was a nice place and the food had not given us any problems before. But you can never be sure in India.

Gooch blamed it on the extra plate of prawns they ordered to accompany the meal; with Gatt we could only narrow it down to one of the 36 dishes he had consumed. Only joking, Gatt – although I'll never forget those hotel suppers in your room, feasting on the cheese, Branston pickle and red wine you had ordered through the British High Commission. Whatever, the captain was clearly out of the reckoning the following morning while Gatt and Robin Smith were eventually forced to leave the field feeling unwell. In the meantime, I had been called in.

My feelings? Just like the one-day international at Lord's. I had worked virtually all my life to play cricket for England and now I had finally made it. A place among the all-time list of Test cricketers. There is an open sewer running down one side of the ground at Madras and in 90 degrees of heat with a crosswind blowing in the wrong direction, it wasn't the most glamorous venue to don the England cap for the first time. But on 11 February 1993, I didn't give a damn.

The match? I didn't concede a single bye as India totted up 560 for 6 declared. In our first innings, I was unlucky, dragging one out of the rough on to my leg and then the stumps. Second time around, I made six before Kumble's extra pace trapped me leg before. We were all out for 252 and the game was lost horribly by an innings and 22. After going down in the first Test in Calcutta, that was it for the three-match series.

In the next match in Bombay, we batted first and were bowled out for 347. They piled up 591 and then rolled us over for 229. Kumble got me both times, for one and nought. Both times he was through me before I moved, one of those startled rabbit jobs. As I walked in, I could almost hear the 'I told you so' jibes from the critics who opposed my selection. The whole party was engulfed in an air of doom and gloom.

I went back to my hotel room; a single. It was a pretty desolate place. I was lonely, disappointed and felt a million miles away from home. No wonder there were tears as I pondered my brief Test career. I had set off with such high hopes but there I was, ten weeks into the tour, and I had managed just three games and five innings. Apart from a couple of one-dayers, when I recorded a 'did not bat' and another duck, that was it for me until we returned home from the Tour from Hell.

Since then, I've never been given another opportunity, never really been mentioned as a possible England player. Some people are given plenty of chances before they are discarded, others disappear off the face of the earth after one or two appearances. Sadly, I fell into the second category. All right, I didn't take my chances in India. But down the years, many players have fared just as badly as me and gone on to play a lot of Test cricket. And I have to say that's very, very disappointing.

But don't run away with the idea that India was three months of unremitting misery. Far from it. The tour never had the atmosphere of my two trips with England A but there were good times as well as bad and, above all, India was a tremendous experience. For until you visit a Third World country, see it, touch it, smell it for yourself, you can never appreciate how different life can be. I have some indelible memories . . .

Like the cricket fans. I have never experienced such fanatical followers. Poke your nose out of the team hotel and there would be a sea of faces, thousands of them, just waiting for a sighting, trying to attract your attention or touch you. They love their cricket and they are very knowledgeable. They would recognise all the England players instantly and I honestly believe that even now, six years after my tour, I would be recognised as an England cricketer if I walked through the streets of Bombay or Delhi. I'm not totally convinced I would receive the same recognition in Barnsley.

Like the smog in Calcutta. It hangs over the city like a huge grey cloud. When we arrived at the ground on the first morning of the Test at Eden Park, we couldn't see out as far as the middle. It was like a thick English winter fog. The start was delayed until the sun burned it away. Particles of smog hang in the air. You breathe the stuff in all day and end up coughing like a 20 cigarettes-a-day man when you wake up in the morning. For two or three months after I got home, my chest felt tight every morning.

Like the Calcutta buses. Imagine the oldest, most clapped-out vehicle over here, churning out black exhaust fumes – and that's what you've got hundreds of times over. Sometimes you can't see across the road after two buses have passed one another.

Like the rivers. In the space of 50 yards they would be used as a toilet, a bath, a laundry, a water supply, a washing-up bowl.

Like the Taj Mahal. A once-in-a-lifetime experience despite the five-hour taxi drive from Delhi, weaving around the roads trying to avoid cows, goats and anything else that had strayed on to the highway, not to mention the exhaust fumes from all the other vehicles.

Like the non-stop supply of bottled water and boiled food. I stuck mainly to rice, or lentils and avoided salads like the plague because there was no way of knowing what they had been washed in. Unlike many of my team-mates, I contrived to avoid a serious attack of the dreaded Delhi Belly.

Like the cockroach that attacked me in Bangalore. I was rooming with Paul Jarvis, a Yorkshire team-mate in those days, and we had settled down for the night when I felt a little tickle on my leg. I put my hand down to scratch it – and felt an insect running up my leg and right up my body. I threw the covers back and switched on the lights to reveal the biggest cockroach you are ever likely to see.

I was out of bed in a flash, looking for something to attack it with. Jarve grabbed one of his boots and we gave chase as the cockroach headed for safety across the room. Paul got there first, though, and after a brief but ferocious struggle, succeeded in flattening the beast with his size ten.

In the same game, our physio Dave Roberts, or Rooster as he is known, was away on the far side of the ground, treating an injured player. Job done, he set off back to the pavilion and we couldn't work out why he suddenly broke into a sprint that would not have shamed Carl Lewis, ducking and weaving as he sped towards us. We soon found out why. When he departed, he was wearing a smart red, white and blue England tracksuit; when he returned he was covered in everything from samosas, bits of chicken curry, chupattis, flat coca cola. It hadn't been a hostile attack, more a bit of good-natured fun. But Rooster certainly didn't see the amusing side of it.

India provided so many experiences that I will never forget; the good, the bad, the funny, the sad. It's so easy to take our comfortable lifestyle for granted but three months in India brings it home with a bang that there's another world out there.

And despite my disappointments on the field, the umpires who seemed to follow a different set of rules, the heat, the smog, the mosquitoes, the constant precautions about food and water, my tour of India will always have a unique place in my memories.

Yorkshire's Bank Holiday trip to Canterbury is unlikely to feature in quite such glowing terms when Blakey looks back on his playing days. Once again Yorkshire, by no means certain of First Division survival in the National League, turn in a tepid performance and are beaten by the proverbial country mile.

And to think that just up the road, Gloucester were playing Somerset in the NatWest Trophy Final at Lord's. It could so easily have been us. Instead, we are going to have to win our final two National League games, against Leicester and Warwickshire, to be sure of playing First Division cricket next season.

Quite frankly, I have run out of words to describe our one-day performances. After beating Notts in the Championship, we should have been on a high but instead I could sense confidence was way down once again. All I can offer is hard work and commitment in the nets in an effort to put things right.

And whatever fixture computer came up with a Bank Holiday trip to Canterbury must have blown a fuse. We'll get back home tonight at around midnight then it's another of those chuck-everything-in-the-washer blitzes before setting off to Scarborough tomorrow afternoon for the first game of the Festival against Durham on Tuesday. But who knows, the sea air might do us good. It usually does.

CGU National League, Canterbury. 29 August. Yorkshire 161–8 (D. Byas 46) lost to Kent 164–1 by 9 wickets.

YORKSHIRE V DURHAM, SCARBOROUGH. NORTHERN ELECTRIC TROPHY

Tuesday, 31 August. The Scarborough Festival. In its heyday, one of cricket's great social occasions and still a magnet for enthusiasts from all over the country. For the players, though, the days when Scarborough was just a chance to wind down after a long, hard season are a thing of the past. After a brief flirtation with the Festival spirit against Durham, Yorkshire face a crucial Championship match against Kent and a National League clash with Leicestershire that could decide their fate for next season.

There can't be a better place to play cricket than North Marine Road when the sun is shining. And after all the ups and downs of recent weeks, it's great to be back. Today marks the club's 150th anniversary and the start of the 113th Scarborough Festival, although this year's event is very different from the Festival's golden era. Between the Wars and in the years immediately after the Second World War, Scarborough in early September was a time for cricket to take a holiday.

The first-class season was over and some of the greatest players in the world converged on the Yorkshire coast to let their hair down on and off the field. Legendary tales of wine, women and song are still recounted by the older generation in the bars and hotels around the town in Festival week. The touring party usually rounded off its fixtures at North Marine Road and there were big crowds to see games like Gentlemen v Players and T.N. Pearce's XI v the MCC.

When I first started, the Festival still featured games involving teams like Michael Parkinson's World XI, the Yorkshire Exiles, the MCC. But over the years the public's appetite for meaningless friendly matches has waned and with so much international cricket being played around the world, it's impossible to drum up a world line-up that would bring the crowds flocking back. Until recently, there was a four-team, one-day competition which always featured Yorkshire and while there were a few decent games, we could sense the general level of interest was low.

The Festival was even switched away from its traditional September slot for a couple of years to test the water of public interest but this year we're back to the original date with our Championship game against Kent and the National League tussle with Leicester the focal points. There was a women's match yesterday, and today we are taking on Durham in the annual joust for the Northern Electric Trophy, the only true Festival match on the agenda this time. A chance to finally lift a trophy!

Win or lose, though, there's rarely a dull moment at Scarborough, although it must be said that Bobby Chapman, the former Notts all-rounder, will have his own views on that particular verdict. North Marine Road has never had quite the same appeal for Chapman since the day he was shot in the backside while quietly minding his own business down on the third man boundary.

It was a Second XI match so I have to confess that my knowledge of the incident is not first-hand. But it coincided with the Battle of the River Plate in nearby Peasholm Park. For those who are unfamiliar with Scarborough in summertime, one of the more enduring tourist attractions is the re-enactment of the final hours of the German pocket battleship, the *Admiral Graf Spee,* on the boating lake in the aforementioned Peasholm Park, not much more than a six hit away from the Scarborough ground. Politically correct it may not be, but it is extremely popular.

Needless to say, the *Graf Spee's* last stand is accompanied by a considerable amount of noise and smoke and many an unwary batsman has been lured to his demise by the high-powered explosion that marks the start of the show. So when, amid all the racket, a sniper with an air rifle in Trafalgar Square, the terrace behind the south side of the ground, decided to join in the fun and scored a direct hit on Chapman's bum, no one heard the shot.

Chapman felt it, though, and started leaping about like a man possessed. Assuming he had been stung by a wasp, the players were convulsed with laughter at his antics – and it was a while before Chapman could convince anyone about what had actually happened and made a painful return to the pavilion as the strains of Rule Britannia signalled the end of the *Graf Spee*. As far as I am aware the sniper, like the British fleet in the South Atlantic, got away.

A bombardment of a different type took place at Scarborough South Cliff Golf Club three years back when the Press almost brought Peter Hartley's Benefit tournament to a halt. Jack had arranged the event for one of Yorkshire's free days, blissfully unaware that it coincided with the announcement of England's winter tour parties. And when Chris Silverwood was named in the senior squad and Michael Vaughan in the A team, a posse of reporters was despatched for some reaction from the two players. The only problem was that at the relevant time, Spoons and Virgil were wrestling with their slices at South Cliff.

Undeterred, three journalists set off in pursuit. I was one of the early starters and encountered them as they disappeared into the middle distance. And it was patently obvious two of the trio had absolutely no idea about the lay-out of the course or, for that matter, the rules and etiquette of golf.

Several near misses were recorded as they weaved across the fairways and shouts of 'Fore!' and far less polite remarks echoed around the links before they finally ran their first quarry to earth at the furthest point of the course. A bemused Silvers was obliged to put the tournament on hold for ten minutes to give a series of impromptu interviews. Then it was time to locate Michael and the mayhem started all over again. It certainly provided a talking point in the clubhouse afterwards.

Scarborough was also the birthplace of one of the great characters of my early years in the Yorkshire side, pace bowler Simon Dennis. Simon, or Donkey as he was known (and that had nothing to do with the animals on Scarborough beach), was a classic case of an accident waiting to happen.

A more than useful medium-pace swing bowler, Donkey suffered for years from a dodgy ankle. Every morning, 20 minutes before we were due to take the field, he would take out a roll of plaster and start strapping up his ankle. He must have gone through about 100 rolls in a season and I have never worked out to this day how he managed to get his boot on with all the strapping.

Anyway, one day at Scarborough, he went through the time-honoured morning rigmarole, his face a mask of concentration. And he was just about to trot in from third man for his first over when he suddenly selected reverse and headed back into the pavilion at maximum revs.

Another bowler was summoned to take his place while Donkey's bemused team-mates waited for an explanation. Sure enough, Dennis rejoined the fray 15 minutes later, looking rather sheepish. When asked what the hell had been going on, he replied, 'Sorry lads, I bandaged the wrong bloody ankle.'

But that was Donkey. On another occasion, we were setting off on an away trip and Simon was due to travel with Neil Hartley. He arrived at Headingley in Martyn Moxon's car and when Frog had found a parking space, Simon spotted Neil's car across the other side of the car park. So Dennis picked his case out of the boot and hauled it across the car park towards Neil's vehicle . . . without realising that he hadn't fastened it up before leaving home and the contents were now spread across 50 yards of Headingley tarmac.

Donkey didn't have the steadiest of hands, either. One day, not long before the start of play, he realised that one of his bootlaces had come loose and needed re-threading. But it was frayed at one end and for Simon, the task of threading it through the eye in his boot proved a monumental effort in concentration.

Neil Hartley was the first to spot his fumbling attempt and quietly nudged his neighbour, Martyn Moxon. Frog nudged his neighbour and so on until Simon was under the silent scrutiny of a full dressing-room of Yorkshire players. When he suddenly looked up and noticed, his response was unprintable.

Other exploits from Donkey included mowing down a whole line of passengers and their luggage trolleys at Jersey Airport courtesy of a slippery surface and a pair of new leather moccasins, trapping his finger under the seat of a bar stool and upsetting a table full of foaming pints and, after a particularly powerful night out in Bradford, misplacing the bathroom light bulb. I was staying at his flat and staggered off for a pee at around 4 a.m., only to find myself in total darkness when I tried to switch on the toilet light. When I challenged

Simon on the subject the next morning, he had no recollection of removing the bulb or of its whereabouts. It eventually turned up in the egg rack in the fridge.

Of course, another character who will always be inexorably linked with Scarborough and the Festival is David Bairstow, a Yorkshire legend who was never less than 110 per cent value at Scarborough. I've spoken earlier about Bluey's qualities as a player but no one with any knowledge of Yorkshire and English cricket in the '70s and '80s will need reminding that David was also a tremendous character.

Everything Bluey did had to be at 100 mph. Whether it was driving his car or downing pints of Tetley's, he always had to be faster than the next man. He used to set himself records for return trips from away grounds. He'd leap in the car and set off like a bat out of hell, having informed us that he'd made it home in 4hr 13 mins last time and reckoned that with a clear run, he could knock a couple of minutes off that personal best. When we saw him next, he'd say, 'What time did you get home then?' And when we offered a rough estimate, he'd roar with delight and reply, 'What? I'd had three pints in the Duke of Wellington by then!'

As captain he used to enjoy taking a couple of the younger lads for a night out, particularly if they were sampling an away trip for the first time. They were understandably flattered to think that the skipper wanted to spend an evening with them, no doubt discussing cricket and their prospects at great length. Bluey had other ideas. For him it was an excuse for a decent meal and a chance to introduce the younger generation to the social side of the first-class game. By the time they realised their error it was too late and a hangover was already on its way.

There were countless Bairstow stories on the field, too. His appeals were legendary. Once in a Sunday League game at Taunton, Phil Carrick succeeded in luring Jimmy Cook, Somerset's South African overseas man and a very fine player, down the track. He played and missed, Bluey whipped off the bails and thundered out an appeal. It was answered in the affirmative.

That should have been that. But to the bemusement of onlookers, Bluey and Cook appeared to be involved in a game of push and shove. No one could work out what was going on until we realised that the force of David's appeal had been enough to blast his false teeth out of his mouth and under Cook's retreating back foot. When they were eventually retrieved, Bluey gave them a quick dust down, replaced them and prepared to receive the next delivery.

Bairstow suffered more than most from the uneven pitches at Headingley towards the end of his career. Only wicketkeepers really know what it feels like when a ball shoots through and hits the end of an injured finger. But believe me, it hurts! So Bluey was less than impressed with some of the tracks prepared by our former groundsman Keith Boyce.

At the start of every game, Boycie would hand over his pitch to the umpires, amble over to the pavilion and take up his customary place on a bench near the groundsman's shed. If the sun was shining, the old shirt would come off and Keith would prepare to relax and watch a bit of cricket. Bairstow, fully wound up for the first delivery of the match, was less laid back about proceedings and decidedly unimpressed if the opening ball shot through and cracked him on the end of a finger. You could see the steam coming out of his ears. He'd wince, grimace and finally turn towards the recumbent groundsman and bawl out, 'Fuckin' 'ell, Boycie, what sort of fuckin' pitch do you call this?'

And if Boyce's tracks weren't bad enough, David also suffered horrendously at the hands of Peter Hartley's traditional morning stiffness. Jack would usually take the first over of the match, with Bairstow behind the stumps in his pristine whites. But unfortunately for our keeper, Jack tended to require a couple of looseners before he got into his stride. Sure enough, nine times out of ten the first ball would sail down the leg side, prompting Bluey to plunge to his left to pull off a spectacular diving stop. He would surface from his exertions purple in the face, his cap askew and his whites covered in dust – and leaving Jack and the Headingley crowd in no doubts about his opinion of that particular ball. I suspect Jack had the last laugh, though, because no one will ever convince me that he didn't do it on purpose.

Bluey was always a good man to have around on pre-season tours as well. One year we went to Barbados and while we played a bit of cricket, there was a fair amount of partying, too. With David leading the charge. One night we hit the happy hour of half-price drinks in prime form and Bluey went on to devote the whole evening to his old pals Red Stripe and Pina Colada. His final gesture before retiring to his room was to eat a couple of pieces of barbecued chicken.

The next morning, he emerged with one of the all-time great hangovers and crept gingerly towards the breakfast table, looking more than a few degrees below par. And before anyone could remind him about the previous night's exploits, he grunted, 'Fuckin' 'ell, that chicken were off.' Down the years, it's become the standard excuse for a hangover in the Yorkshire dressing-room.

No one who knew Bluey will ever forget him. A super player and a larger-than-life character who always lived life to the full and enjoyed everything connected with the game of cricket on and off the field. Perhaps in the end, he just couldn't cope with a life without cricket. We'll never really know.

Northern Electric Trophy, Scarborough. 31 August. Yorkshire 236–4 (D. Byas 80, A. McGrath 63, G.M. Fellows 58*) beat Durham 145 (McGrath 4–14) by 91 runs.

YORKSHIRE V KENT, SCARBOROUGH

Wednesday, 1 September. There are three Yorkshire players in the England party to tour South Africa this winter, Darren Gough, Gavin Hamilton and Michael Vaughan. Gough, however, faces serious question marks over his fitness after being restricted to just one Championship appearance for Yorkshire since the end of England's involvement in the World Cup three months ago. Hamilton has his injury worries, too. He hobbled out of yesterday's Festival game with Durham with a recurrence of an old hamstring injury and leaves later today for a check-up in Leeds. As his team-mates take the field against Kent, Hamilton, understandably, looks a worried man.

I'm absolutely delighted for Darren, Gavin and Michael. They deserve it. Goughie was always going to be an automatic choice, fitness permitting of course, and no one can dispute Gavin's right to a place, either. He had a marvellous World Cup with Scotland and right now he's in the top ten in both the national batting and bowling averages. You can't argue with figures like that, particularly as most of the players above him are overseas men.

I've made no secret of my admiration for Gav as a cricketer and a person so no one will be keener than me to see him do well. He'll have a laugh with the best of us when we call him our resident dickhead but he's deadly serious about his cricket and I'm convinced he'll do well. I know that deep down he's worried that this hamstring problem is playing him up again and we'll all be glad when he receives the all-clear after his scans. In fact, we'll be keeping our fingers crossed for both of them.

And thankfully the selectors decided to go with class rather than current form and pick Michael. To be blunt, his runs this year don't warrant his selection. Apart from those two centuries down at Chelmsford, he's struggled a bit, particularly at Headingley. We could have done with a bigger contribution from him as our senior opening batsman – and no one knows that better than Virgil himself. But here in Yorkshire we all know what a high-quality player he is and it's good to see the England selectors saying, 'We think he's a class player and we're going to go with him.' That makes a pleasant change.

He had a tremendous A tour last year both as captain and batsman, returning with the Future England Captain mantle worn by Mike Atherton at the start of the '80s. And there's no reason why Michael can't go all the way. He's worked tremendously hard to make himself a more than useful off-spin bowler and his fielding has improved out of all recognition. He has a good tactical brain and is widely regarded as the heir apparent to David Byas here in Yorkshire. I don't think any of the lads would argue with that.

I can pay him no higher compliment than to call him a good Yorkshire lad. And considering he was born in Manchester, that's some accolade. When he first arrived on the scene it was widely assumed that he was a university lad because he does have a rather studious air about him. But the nearest he got to the academic world was seven GCSE's at Silverdale Comprehensive in Sheffield. He's a down-to-earth guy who enjoys his nights out and his football – and we won't hold it against him that he supports Sheffield Wednesday. I suppose it's just a cross he has to bear. Actually he's not a bad footballer himself and turns out for his local side in one of the Sheffield leagues. He'll have to give it a miss this winter, though.

It looks as if Chris Silverwood won't be around either – but instead of taking his place on the England tour, the word is he'll be given the consolation prize of an A tour to Bangladesh and New Zealand.

And you really have to feel sorry for Spoons. He's performed exceptionally well for two years now. He's an honest, hardworking professional with a big, big heart who always gives it 110 per cent. He'll run in all day long if you ask him. He moves the ball mainly back into the batsman and I suppose if you're being choosy, a bit more away movement would help him get the really top players out. But his extreme pace does the business more often than not.

He's deserved an opportunity in the Test arena this summer and there can be no doubt that he has been treated very shabbily by the England hierarchy. He was called up for the first Test against New Zealand on the back of some outstanding county performances. Then, after impressing everyone in the England practice sessions, he was left out of the final eleven.

He didn't even make the squad for the second game but returned for the last two and was left out of both matches. Each time he was omitted, he was led to understand he would be chosen next time. Then when Ed Giddins got the nod ahead of him in the last Test, he set off home believing he would definitely be on the main tour. Instead he's missed out. On top of all that, his wife was injured in that car crash before the NatWest semi-final so, one way or another, it's not been much of a year for Spoons.

But you wouldn't know it. He's kept his spirits up and he'll just keep plugging away. He's already toured Zimbabwe and New Zealand in 1996–97 and the West Indies in 1997–98, winning his only England cap in the process. And his chance will come again. As he's a karate black belt, it might be an idea to pick him sooner rather than later . . . before he gets cross.

At least he can get rid of his frustrations by riding off into the sunset on his high-powered motor bike. Both he and Craig White, another player who has reason to feel aggrieved after missing out on the one-day squad for South Africa, are motor bike fanatics. Fast bowlers, fast machines.

They come sweeping into the ground in their crash helmets and leathers and if ever there's a break in play on an away trip, off they go in search of the local bike shop to check out the goodies. If you catch them having a chat in a corner of the den, you can guarantee the topic of conversation won't be cricket equipment. They'll be discussing new leathers, riding gloves or helmets; finding out where they went for a spin last night. It's got so bad that instead of picking up a top-shelf magazine to peruse during a quiet moment or two, the lads find themselves reading *Motor Cycle News* or some other bikers' publication.

Chalkie reckons he can cut 20 minutes to half an hour off his journey to and from Scarborough – and given the state of the traffic on the A64, I can well believe it. He arrives at the ground, parks his pride and joy in a prime position where he can keep a close eye on it and then strides into the dressing-room looking like The Terminator. Woe betide anyone who even contemplates letting his tyres down, although I have to admit the thought has crossed my mind. It would probably be enough to drive him back to Australia.

Still, good luck to them, even though their hobby might be a bit on the dangerous side for most of us. In fact, you won't catch me within a million miles of the pillion seat when either of our budding TT aces is on board.

Vaughan responds to his selection with a high-class innings of 153 as Yorkshire score their second successive Championship victory on the best cricket pitch they have seen all season. Silverwood's response to his omission from the England tour is match figures of 9 for 114. He also underlines his growing batting prowess with a hard-hitting, unbeaten half century in the first innings. Blakey, finally promoted in the batting order, does not fare as well, scoring nought in the first innings and 15 second time around.

Glorious Scarborough weather, a super pitch, big crowds and an emphatic five-wicket win on the final afternoon. The game ebbed and flowed from the first morning and even the defeated Kent players acknowledged they had been involved in a superb match. This is what Championship cricket is supposed to be all about.

The bowlers had to work bloody hard and bowl well for their wickets and almost to a man they responded, making life difficult for most of the batsmen with the exception of Virgil and Dick Harden, who put together the crucial partnership of the match by adding 147 for the sixth wicket in our first knock.

After batting at four in the game against Durham, I held on to the job against Kent. I was desperate to do well and justify David's faith in me. Instead I finished the match with 15 runs from two innings and the feeling that I had let him down. I've waited a hell of a long time for this chance and now I will just have to hope the skipper sticks with me for the game against Glamorgan at Headingley next week. Logically, he will. It hardly seems fair to discard me from the top order again after just one chance. But you never know. After all, Dick finally came good here and he will be fancying his chances of a move back up the order, too. Unsettling.

PPP Healthcare County Championship. Scarborough. 1–4 September. Yorkshire 389 (M.P. Vaughan 153, R.J. Harden 64, C.E.W. Silverwood 53*) and 141–5 (Vaughan 50) beat Kent 302 (M.A. Ealham 59, Silverwood 5–67) and 226 (E.T. Smith 55, Silverwood 4–57) by 5 wickets.

YORKSHIRE PHOENIX V LEICESTERSHIRE FOXES, SCARBOROUGH. NATIONAL LEAGUE

Sunday, 5 September. With less than a fortnight to go before the curtain is brought down on another season, plans for the first campaign of the new millennium are already starting to take shape. Yorkshire will break new ground next year with a pre-season tour to Australia, spending three weeks of the English winter based in Perth. Nice work if you can get it – and a million miles away from those pre-season routines of Blakey's early career. In recent years, all the first-class counties have joined the trend of spending a few weeks in the sun to prepare, physically and mentally, for the new campaign. Yorkshire have visited the Caribbean, Zimbabwe and South Africa.

Australia 2000 will be my 22nd overseas tour of one sort or another. I've toured at all levels with England, with Yorkshire and with some unofficial parties. And yes, I know exactly how lucky I have been to play cricket in some of the loveliest parts of the world. Places like South Africa, Zimbabwe, the West Indies and now a return to Australia, where I spent three winters playing Grade cricket in Melbourne.

In the final analysis, of course, pre-season tours are not just a paid holiday. Cricket comes first. So while you can't beat the West Indies for its beaches and social life, it has to be said that the cricketing side could be better. The net facilities are a bit iffy and you can never be certain about whether the transport will arrive to take the team to matches and back to the hotel.

In fact, you can't totally guarantee that the opposition will turn up. In Antigua in 1994, we found ourselves all dressed up with no one to play – although our opponents' absence might just have had something to do with a Test match between England and the West Indies being played down the road in St Johns in which a certain Brian Lara scored 375. As I recall, we were not too upset about the match-off decision because it meant we had a free day languishing on the beach. But it wasn't exactly the way to prepare for a new season.

South Africa is a different world. Everything from transport to hotels to practice facilities is A1 and some of the cricket is played on Test grounds. I'm sure Australia will be just as good.

But pre-season touring is not all about cricket. After a winter apart, there's also a strong element of team-building and it will be no surprise to learn that down the years we have enjoyed a vivid social scene, too. I can modestly reveal that, as the team's official social secretary, I have regularly played a leading role in raising morale for the season ahead.

And it isn't just about wining and dining. The social committee always tries to introduce sporting activities, too. We once organised a tennis tournament in the West Indies and Simon Kellett, who fancied himself as a bookmaker, decided to take a few bets. We heard him muttering things like: 'Blakey – he can run a bit . . . 8–1. Hartley – natural ball player . . . 10–1. Byas – farmer . . . no chance. 25–1.' Little did he know!

Most of the lads can spot a good bet when they see one and inevitably the rank outsider attracted considerable interest. And as Bingo eased himself to the final without losing a game, the colour gradually drained from Simon's sun-tanned features. David's eventual victory cost our very own William Hill around $1,200 and earned Bingo a lap of honour around the court.

And then there were the Yorkshire Olympics, which took place on the idyllic Caribbean beaches of Anguilla a few years back. Held over two weeks, the Olympics featured various events on the beach outside the hotel and the real highlight was always going to be the Sumo wrestling competition.

It was held on an afternoon off and we used the hotel mini-buses to head off to a quieter beach. There was much hilarity when the draw was made, not least because one of the bouts pitted me against Colin Chapman, our reserve wicketkeeper. I lost. But the main attraction was clearly going to be the heavyweight tussle between Peter Hartley and Alex Wharf, who moved to Notts a couple of seasons ago. A contest to be savoured.

I must admit I was surprised to see the boys taking it so seriously. And while the committee were diligently marking out the circle for the wrestling to take place, the other occupants of the beach were treated to the sight of 13 Yorkshire cricketers oiling themselves up in readiness for the grappling ahead. One or two of the German tourists even started to forget their suntans and take a vague interest in our activities.

I made a formal announcement that the proceedings were about to get under way and that the first bout would be a catchweight contest between Bradley Parker and Matthew Wood. To much cheering and laughter, the two combatants launched the event, watched by their team-mates and an ever-increasing audience of tourists.

So by the time the *pièce de résistance* of Hartley v Wharf was announced, there were almost 100 bemused Germans and quite a few of the locals eagerly awaiting a battle royal. And they weren't disappointed. Wharf weighed in at 6ft 4in. and 15st. 10lb. and Jack at a more modest but no less forbidding 6ft and 14st. 1lb. To roars of encouragement in English and German, they set to – and a titanic struggle ensued. Jack won the first of the three rubbers but Wharfie levelled in the second. So it was everything to grapple for in the final. Fortunes ebbed and flowed until, with two enormous grunts, the pair collapsed in a heap on the floor. Jack was on top at the time so he was adjudged the winner.

Alex took it in good part. And it wasn't until he returned to his room and the adrenaline started to wear off that he began to feel a bit sore around the ribcage. Sure enough, Jack's final heave had left him nursing a cracked rib and we had to spend the next couple of weeks covering up for him. The official line in the press back home in Yorkshire was that he had been hit by a short delivery in the nets. From Jack, of course.

That particular tour was one of those rare occasions when Dave Byas allowed his professional standards to slip – for once. Bingo is the most professional cricketer I have ever met. He is never, repeat never, late for practice, training, nets or a match. And surrounded by the delights of Anguilla, he still insisted on a strict fitness regime. If we had a spare half hour, we would be away down the beach for a run or some interval training.

As a farmer, Dave is used to rising early so it was no big deal for him when he ordered a 6 a.m. start on the beach for an Iron Man run and swim competition – on our day off. It went down like a lead balloon with the rest of the boys but we bit the bullet, had a relatively early night and duly reported for our dawn fitness drill.

But where was the captain? Five, ten, fifteen, twenty minutes went by before we spotted a familiar figure gingerly making his way down the hotel steps and on to the beach. Dave was clearly suffering but, incredibly, managed to perform to his usual high standards even though he had fallen among thieves the night before and found himself in the middle of a major drinking school. He wasn't allowed to forget it for the rest of the tour.

He exacted full revenge the following year on a three-week trip to Zimbabwe. We worked incredibly hard on the cricketing side in the first and last weeks but the middle week was designated as a team-building exercise. We had a couple of days at Victoria Falls and then moved on to a safari lodge in Botswana. It was supposed to be a relaxing break – but our leader deemed otherwise and, sure enough, organised a heavy-duty training work-out for us.

We split into two groups, one half heading off on mountain bikes and the rest swimming and exercising around the pool. When the cyclists returned after half an hour or so, roles would be reversed. I was in the second group and as Dave led the bikers out into the bush, we went through the motions with a few press-ups and exercises before devoting the rest of the session to swimming. An hour went by, and then another and as dark began to fall, we started to worry.

Eventually we spotted a solitary figure pumping away at the pedals in the direction of the lodge – Byas. He had barely broken sweat and stayed in the saddle throughout. The same could hardly be said of the rag-tag army who followed him into the hotel in a state of near-exhaustion. The leisurely bike ride around the block had turned into a nightmare journey across impossible terrain. Most of the lads ended up humping their bikes on to their shoulders and trying not to notice snake tracks and elephant droppings as they headed back to base.

The second group reckoned we had got off pretty lightly, until Bingo decided to repeat the exercise the following morning . . . with a combined cycle and run over the same route in the afternoon. The morning was every bit as bad as we feared but we survived somehow. Then came the afternoon. Eight runners, eight cyclists, a guide in a Ford Escort van – and a pack of baboons. Unfriendly.

At first it was just one or two. But we gradually realised 40 or 50 had gathered and were closing in on us, making some extremely menacing noises in the process. Byas was all for going on. But the rest of the lads had long since decided enough was enough. A 15–1 majority voted in favour of a return to the lodge, the Escort van was summoned and eight mountain bikes and 16 Yorkshire cricketers piled aboard to beat an undignified but grateful retreat. To make matters worse, we subsequently discovered we had strayed off the beaten track and shouldn't have been there in the first place. That's no doubt what the baboons were trying to tell us.

This year, Bingo's little treat featured Table Mountain and another 6 a.m. start. We gathered in the foyer of our hotel to be informed that we would be going up Table Mountain for breakfast. Fair enough. It was only when we piled out of our mini buses at base camp that we realised the cable cars didn't start until 7 a.m. Two hours of non-stop climbing ensued. After our much-needed meal, Dave at least allowed us the luxury of a cable car back down – where we encountered the hire bikes for our journey back to the hotel. I dread to think what he'll have in store for us in Perth. Shark wrestling, perhaps.

I suppose, after listening to these tales, some people will accuse us of being a bunch of grown-up kids. And the sight of Dick Harden marking his tour début with an impersonation of Baby Spice would have done little to change that view. But it's vital to build a good spirit and learn what makes the other players tick. And having fun is all part of the process.

There's plenty of fun for the spectators at North Marine Road, too, as Yorkshire, watched by a crowd of over 6,000, finally reproduce their early-season National League form and demolish Leicestershire with something to spare to end a two-month drought and a run of seven successive defeats.

A super performance. The boys bowled consistently, batted positively and fielded like stags. Can we bottle this up and save it for Lord's finals and NatWest semi-finals, please?

CGU National League, Scarborough. 5 September. Yorkshire Phoenix 142–3 beat Leicestershire Foxes 139 by 7 wickets.

YORKSHIRE V GLAMORGAN, HEADINGLEY

Wednesday, 8 September. The final home game of the season. And for three members of the Yorkshire staff, it's a traumatic occasion. Batsman Bradley Parker, all-rounder Gareth Clough and off-spinner Richard Wilkinson have been told that their services will no longer be required.

A hammer blow for all three. At this time of year there are always reports of casualties around the county circuit but it hits hardest when the players concerned occupy seats in your own dressing-room.

Gareth has made just one first-class appearance while Richard has yet to appear in the senior line-up. They started the season with dreams of progressing into the Yorkshire side; now they find themselves looking for a job. At 21, they are both young enough and talented enough to find another club but there are a lot of players out there in a similar plight and I just hope against hope that it works out for them.

But it's a whole new ball game for Bradley. Nest, as we call him because of the state of his hair, was one of the first intake into our Academy in 1989. He turned pro three years later and has since played in 44 Championship games, averaging 30-plus. And he's been a more than useful one-day performer, too. So he hasn't done badly by any means.

But he has never really established himself and now, at 29, the powers-that-be have decided he's expendable. I think Nestie was expecting it but it's still a massive blow. He's been a good guy to have around and a huge character in the dressing-room with his practical jokes and booming laugh. He has to be a contender for the Phantom Sock Snipper and his absence from the side on a regular basis this year reinforces the view that he could be our man.

I don't know what he'll do now. Neither does he, I suppose. I just hope things work out for him. It must have been tough playing Second XI cricket this year but he has never complained. Down the years, though, a lot of players have been left to wish they had made serious plans for the future by spending their winters training for another career. And many players end up regretting not acting earlier. You get hired and fired and in the end, what have you got to show for it?

I am keenly aware that this is going to happen to me one day, too, although I have every intention of being around for a few years yet. I'm fit enough and as long as Yorkshire want me and I know I can do myself justice, I'll stick around. Fitness and motivation have never been a problem. Deep down, I have always wanted to play in a Yorkshire Championship-winning side and the challenge is still there.

Even so, I like to think I've got my finger on the pulse as far as my future is concerned. The winters I have spent working for Media Works have given me an insight into the world of marketing and PR. At first, I was taken on board mainly as a front man, whose sporting contacts with the business world would help to open a few doors for the company. But as time has progressed I have started to play a much more active role. I enjoy it a lot and it's something I am looking to develop.

I also have my own leisurewear business, Richard Blakey Leisure. It started in a very small way, supplying a few cricket clubs with some clothing and tracksuits. Now we have taken some hockey and football clubs on board as well and also moved into the corporate market.

My dad keeps it ticking over. Without him it would be impossible. Down the years, he and mum have given me tremendous support. I suppose no one realises as a youngster how much their parents have sacrificed. You just take for granted that you will have all the gear, that you will be able to turn up on time for trials and nets, that there will always be someone there to turn to for support and encouragement.

I suppose my parents were forewarned about my long-term intentions when they used to look out of the window early in the morning in the school holidays to see me mowing a wicket in the back garden. I worked long hours to prepare a white track like the ones I saw on the telly and when dad got home from work, I would be padded up and ready for the first session. Then we would play on for another couple of hours after the tea interval until bad light stopped play. I lost count of the greenhouse and kitchen windows that had to be replaced.

I even went as far as having my own set of covers and as soon as the rain started, I would grab a few old sheets and blankets and dash out to put them on my lovingly prepared wicket. I failed to appreciate, of course, that they were not exactly first-class quality and when the rain stopped I would be batting on a seamer's paradise.

Over the last couple of years or so, I have received tremendous support from Clare, too. I've said earlier that cricket is not the ideal environment to build and sustain relationships. For six months of the year, you hardly see your partner and inevitably when he is around, cricket and everything that goes with it dominates his life. My first marriage suffered from the same strains and stresses that have affected so many players down the years, but Clare has come to terms with what's involved and I couldn't ask for a more ideal partner.

By the time Yorkshire's game against Glamorgan draws to a close, Blakey is wrestling with a dilemma: whether to laugh or cry. Tears are definitely in order after a diabolical Yorkshire performance that sees the Welshmen, certainties for Second Division cricket next year, cruise to an innings victory. Yet for Blakey, once again batting at number four, the game becomes a personal triumph as he scores his first century for three seasons, helping Yorkshire's second innings to recover from the ignominy of 11 for 2 to the relative respectability of 306 all out.

I'm not pretending one innings has changed my life and I know as well as the next man that a week is a long time in cricket. But after this century, I feel a different person. More confident, more upbeat. Having that extra responsibility of batting at the top of the order has changed my whole approach. I feel a million dollars about my batting again. A huge weight has been lifted from my shoulders.

I won't get carried away but if I can finish by scoring a few runs in Sunday's one-dayer against Warwickshire and our final Championship game against Surrey at The Oval I will, at the very least, have reminded people out there that Richard Blakey can still do it. I will have prompted a few questions about the batting line-up next year. And hopefully I will figure more prominently than I have this time.

Even after failing twice in the last game at Scarborough, I felt confident coming into this one. And while this opportunity in the top four was not exactly the last chance saloon, you don't have to be a genius to work out that if I blew it, there might not be another opportunity for a long time.

I batted well for my 20 in the first innings before getting caught at short leg off a ball that bounced a bit more than I anticipated. But in the second innings it just felt right from the word go. The rest of the boys were giving off bad vibes about the state of the pitch but I never really encountered any problems at all. Nor, as it happens, did the Glamorgan players as they compiled 498.

One or two deliveries misbehaved when the ball was new and it was pretty hard work. But it was never a bag of snakes. I got on with the job in hand and didn't really have any worries until the ninth wicket went down with me still six short of three figures. The sight of Ryan Sidebottom emerging from the pavilion with the scoreboard reading Blakey 94 was not totally encouraging but, all credit to him, he played magnificently for his 48.

I progressed to 99 and was grateful to be facing Robert Croft rather than Jacques Kallis on that track. I turned Croftie down to fine leg, ran the first one fast and came back for the second. I'd done it! The first feeling was jubilation, waving to the players' balcony and acknowledging the crowd's applause. Then relief. It was only another run, from 99 to 100. But after three long years and a slide down the order, that one run means so much. We went on to post 78 for the last wicket before I was last man out for 123. One, two three. Yes, I'd certainly accept any of those slots in the order next season.

And from a personal point of view, a great day all round. I hit a ton and Clare arrived home full of the joys of spring to tell me she's landed a new job in the commercial department at Leeds Rhinos Rugby League club. We didn't need an excuse to go out for a nice meal and a few drinks.

PPP Healthcare County Championship, Headingley. 8–11 September. Yorkshire 140 and 306 (R.J. Blakey 123) lost to Glamorgan 498 (M.P. Maynard 186) by an innings and 52 runs.

YORKSHIRE PHOENIX V WARWICKSHIRE BEARS, HEADINGLEY. NATIONAL LEAGUE

Sunday, 12 September. The end of the season is near as Yorkshire play their final home game, needing victory to guarantee a place in next year's National League First Division. The game also marks the end of an era in White Rose cricket. After 50 years as player and coach, Doug Padgett has decided to step down.

A lovely man, Doug. And what an incredible record – 50 years with one club. He's given his life to Yorkshire cricket and it will be an emotional moment when he finally says farewell at a reception at Headingley tomorrow night.

He's been a huge influence on so many Yorkshire players since he joined the coaching staff in 1971 after a playing career which brought him 20,306 first-class runs and a couple of England caps. Recently he's been involved with the Second XI, which is where I first encountered him 15 years ago.

He helped me a lot in those early days and I have always listened to his advice. Doug was never a man to rant and rave but he could see instantly if there was something not quite right and would take me quietly to one side and show me where I was going wrong. He also believed in leaving well alone if things were going smoothly, a quality that some of the so-called high-profile coaches might be advised to adopt. I owe him a lot.

But it isn't just his coaching skills that we will all miss. For despite his quiet, unassuming image, Doug has a superb sense of humour and enjoys nothing more than a good dressing-room prank, particularly with the younger lads.

One of his favourites was to take one of the boys aside before a game against Glamorgan in Wales and remind him to take his passport. This was always greeted with a look of disbelief but Doug would insist and when none of the other players, most of whom had seen it all before, argued the toss, the new boy would inevitably start to wonder. He'd double check with a couple of his team-mates, ask Doug again and then eventually play safe and bring his passport along.

And, without a word of a lie, there was one priceless occasion when the young player on the wrong end of Doug's trick finally confessed to his mentor that he didn't have the necessary paperwork for the trip to the Principality. He'd left his passport at home. It was the moment Padge had been waiting for. 'Don't worry, lad,' he said. 'You travel with me and I'll see you're all right.'

Sure enough, when the pair were within half a mile or so of the Welsh border, Doug pulled the car to the side of the road, ordered the bemused lad out of the passenger seat and instructed him to climb into the boot. 'Just stay quiet until we're safely across the other side and then I'll get you out,' whispered Padge. He then motored quietly along for a couple of minutes before rolling to a halt, sharing a conversation with an imaginary border guard and resuming his journey. Safely round the next corner, he stopped, opened the boot and released his illegal but very relieved immigrant.

Doug was usually in charge of eating arrangements on the Second XI grounds and would delight in telling the lads that it was boiled fish for lunch, never a popular choice. 'T'chef says there's five portions of steak and kidney pie left over from yesterday, though, but you'll have to order it specially when you've got your kit on. It's first come, first served.' This would prompt a furious rush to get changed and a dash for the kitchen in pursuit of a decent lunch. Needless to say, the steak and kidney pie, not to mention the boiled fish, was a figment of Doug's imagination.

Sometimes he would catch a junior pro out with his collection trick. When a player scores 50 or takes five wickets in the leagues, his team-mates go around the ground with a cap and the punters drop in a few coppers to show their appreciation. So once in a while, when a Second

XI player reached the 50-mark, Doug would call a youngster over, hand him a cap and tell him to do the collection. Baffled spectators would reluctantly part with their hard-earned brass – only to have it returned to them when Padge came clean and admitted it was just a joke.

Doug was usually one of the first to arrive at the ground in the morning and would station himself in a corner of the dressing-room, armed with a newspaper and a cup of tea, as the kids wandered in. Inevitably, tales of the previous night's sexual exploits would be recounted and Doug, pretending to read his paper, would listen in with one ear, a wry, knowing smile on his face. Eventually, when proceedings started to get a bit too bawdy for a man of his years, Doug would haul himself to his feet, pick up his paper and wander off in the direction of another cuppa, musing, 'A standing cock has no conscience.' It was one of his favourite sayings.

We'll miss him a lot. He's been very loyal to Yorkshire cricket and the players down the years and a good man to have around. I'm certain he'll be able to take some time out from watching Bradford City to come and see us next year and I hope he has a happy retirement.

Which, as it happens, is what some people have been wishing me lately. It's one of three pieces of speculation currently doing the rounds. First of all, I'm supposed to be retiring at the end of the season. Then I'm about to be appointed Second XI captain. And finally, I'll be giving up the gloves next season and opening the batting. Quite where these rumours start, I don't know.

The idea about a new batting role is reasonable enough, I suppose. I've never disguised my wish to bat higher up the order, of course, and after my 100 against Glamorgan, there has been renewed talk in the press that I might relinquish my wicketkeeping duties and go in first next season. But there has been nothing official from either Martyn or David. As I mentioned earlier, I'll be talking to them in the next week or ten days to see what they have in mind for me but at this stage I would be very reluctant to give up wicketkeeping.

I have had absolutely no indication that I am being considered as a possible Second XI captain, though, and I can categorically state that rumours of my imminent retirement are, to say the least, premature. Not to mention bewildering and upsetting. Quite frankly, if I could get my hands on the people who started that particular flier, I would waste no time in demonstrating that I am not always the quiet, laid back character people see out in the middle.

Away from the rumour factory, though, Blakey has another good day as Yorkshire banish the spectre of relegation from the National League in front of almost 10,000 fans. He follows an undefeated 34, sharing a stand of 75 with Byas, by claiming five victims behind the stumps, three caught and two stumped. It is a haul that brings his tally for the season to 32, a new record in what was once the Sunday League and is now the National League.

As I always said about wicketkeeping records, if the bowlers don't hit the edge, I don't get the catches. But while I won't be trumpeting this one from the rooftops, it's nice to be mentioned in despatches again. As far as the team is concerned, another flawless performance. Just like last week's game against Leicestershire at Scarborough. We grabbed the match by the scruff of the neck, every department fired on all cylinders and we won with plenty to spare. Quality!

CGU National League, Headingley. 12 September. Yorkshire Phoenix 238–3 (D. Byas 67, M.P. Vaughan 56) beat Warwickshire Bears 210 (D.P. Ostler 52, M.J. Powell 51, C. White 4–39) by 28 runs.

SURREY V YORKSHIRE, THE OVAL

The final game of a disappointing campaign which started with such high hopes back in April. Yorkshire head south aiming to deny new champions Surrey, one of their oldest rivals, the rare distinction of an unbeaten record in the County Championship. It's time to load up the car for the last time, to check the route to The Oval and then lock into the daily round and common task that makes up a first-class player's season.

I try to be at the ground a couple of hours before the start of play so, with the 10.30 a.m. start at this time of year, that means being on the road early. But with the usual 11 a.m. start, I'm up around 7 o'clock. I never, ever miss breakfast – almost always it's cereals and toast, which are both slow-burning carbohydrates, juice and tea. Maybe I'll also have some scrambled eggs or baked beans. On away trips, with a hot buffet on offer, there's a big temptation to dig into the full breakfast and some of the lads always fall by the wayside, particularly the fast bowlers.

I leave home or the hotel with plenty of time to spare in case of traffic problems and after checking my mail or making any calls, I'm ready for a team warm-up at 9.30 a.m. It's been an essential part of my regime for the whole of my career. It's vital to do everything humanly possible to stay fit, physically and mentally, and I believe a proper warm-up helps. Afterwards we'll have a net and I may get my eye in by keeping to the spinners for a while. These days, I never warm up with the fast bowlers, though, because I need to protect my hands. That's the reason you won't see me taking throws during fielding practice.

We like to be back in the den half an hour before the start of play for another cup of tea, to take a bit more liquid on board and give ourselves a chance to collect our thoughts. When play starts, you won't find all the players on the batting side sitting glued to the cricket, although having said that, I reckon it gives off the right vibes if the team is seen to be supporting the two guys out in the middle. But it's impossible to watch every ball, as this would sap most of the concentration we will need for batting. To relax, people down the order find time to have a look at the papers, maybe work out in the gym, sort out any personal loose ends there may be. If it's a Tuesday, I'll polish up my *Huddersfield Examiner* column. We always have one eye or ear on the play, though, and I start to concentrate properly two or three wickets before I'm due to go in. In the last couple of games, that has meant from the start of the innings.

Food-wise, will eat according to the state of the game. Sometimes I will have something light, with plenty more liquid, or maybe have a bigger meal. At the close of play, it's drinks all-round. And how that order has changed! When I first started it was bitter or lager . . . and 12 foaming pints would be waiting for us as we dragged ourselves back into the dressing-room. Now it's one pint of Guinness and eleven soft drinks. The black stuff is for the captain, who likes nothing better than a cigarette and a refreshing pint to help him mull over the day's events.

Ten years or more ago, we would usually head off to the pub for a few pints afterwards but again, times have changed. On away trips, I might pop out for a couple of beers but when we're at Headingley, I'll just go home for a bite to eat, usually around 8.30 p.m., and an early night. I really must be getting old! We virtually never go out socially during a game . . . the last thing I want is for a few punters to see me having a quiet drink in the pub with Clare or a few friends. One pint of lager would be transformed into a gallon of ale and anything less than 100 per cent perfection the following day would be blamed on my excessive drinking habits.

And late nights have a nasty habit of rebounding on you. One year, the lads arrived at Scarborough on the eve of a Festival game to be greeted by horrendous weather. The forecast was for more of the same for the next 48 hours so they pressed the gamble button and hit the town. Gales were still lashing the east coast when they returned to the hotel in the wee small hours. So, confident there would be no action the following day, they appointed one of their number to check the weather at 8 a.m. – just in case – and retired to bed.

The first alarm call was heard at 8.01 a.m., followed by muffled curses of disbelief all down the hotel corridor. The sun was already beating down, reflecting off the mill pond otherwise known as the North Sea, and holidaymakers were out early, strolling around in their shirtsleeves. As I had arrived at the hotel late the previous evening and decided to give the bunfight a miss, I was able to view the subsequent proceedings with considerable amusement.

Having said that, I'll enjoy a good night out with the best of them – like next Wednesday at Headingley. Our end-of-season bash. It's always a good do and one year we went completely over the top and took ourselves off to Dublin for a couple of nights. It ended disastrously with a paint-balling match, organised by Goughie, against some very mean looking Irishmen. We surrendered early in the proceedings.

And arguably the most memorable of our end-of-season parties was at Scarborough in 1993. I decreed that it would be a Roman evening and all the lads duly turned up wearing a toga. Richie Richardson looked magnificent so he was immediately crowned Caesar. Every time he stood up, the whole company would rise, stand on their chairs and bellow, 'Hail Caesar!' Richie rose to the occasion magnificently, of course, and can still claim to be the only Roman emperor to sport Oakley sunglasses.

The match and the longest season on record end in anti-climax as bad light halts play on the final afternoon with Surrey 57 for 4 in pursuit of 201. The size of their victory target is due in no small part to Blakey's second innings of 70 in which he shares a seventh wicket partnership of 84 with Ian Fisher. His season ends with a 100 per cent appearance record in all forms of cricket, 684 first-class runs at an average of 25.33 and 41 victims behind the stumps. But it's been a long haul.

Physically, I'm completely knackered. Two dodgy knees, a dodgy ankle and my hands are hanging together by a thread. My left hand has never recovered from the dislocated finger I collected at Scarborough in July and I damaged the right hand in the game against Glamorgan last week. Every time I take a ball that doesn't go into the gloves clean it's absolute purgatory. But overall, I've done OK, even though it's been a case of just getting through each game since I dislocated the finger. I suppose I could have played the sympathy card and told the world I was struggling. But that's not the way I play my cricket.

We've been on the road for nearly 22 weeks and 39 games. That's a long time and a lot of cricket. The old timers claim modern players don't know what hard work is but if you look at the figures we play almost as much as they did. Before the one-day revolution, they played 32 three-day Championship games, a scheduled 96 days' cricket irrespective of rainy days and early finishes. This year, we had 17 four-day Championship games and 16 National League matches on the calendar. Plus three Super Cup ties and four games in the NatWest. That's 91 days. We also play longer hours and even the sternest critic of the modern game will admit that the tempo is much higher. So don't blame us for being very tired.

Mentally, though, I would happily go on for another month or so because after finally being given a chance to bat up the order again I know I'm in excellent nick. And with 222 runs in my last four innings it's frustrating, to put it mildly, not to have a few more games to state my case for next season. I'll just have to live with that, I'm afraid. Overall, though, I feel my batting has been better this year. I played some important innings before moving back up the order, although it's never easy batting at eight and nine, particularly in one-day cricket.

For the team, there's no silverware to go on display yet again. That's a massive disappointment. In some counties, sixth place in the Championship, fifth in the National League, a Lord's final and a NatWest semi-final would be regarded as a decent year. Until recently, that would have been the response here in Yorkshire. Not any more. With the ability we have in the squad, a reasonable season is no longer good enough. Expectations are huge.

It would be easy to make excuses, of course. We could point to the injuries that have limited Goughie and Hutch to six matches and 162.3 overs between them. Matthew Hoggard played just eight times.

But the fact is that we have, as the captain says, only played to about 60 per cent of our potential in both Championship and one-day cricket. We haven't scored anything like enough runs and we haven't bowled well enough for long enough to launch a serious challenge for honours. So another frustrating time, and there is a lot of hard thinking to be done before we report back next March.

Next on the agenda for me, though, is a couple of weeks' rest before going back to Media Works for the winter. I'll try to fit in a holiday somewhere along the line. And, of course, there's a book to finish.

PPP Healthcare County Championship, The Oval. 15–18 September. Yorkshire 115 (C.G. Greenidge 5–60) and 213–9 dec. (R.J. Blakey 70, I.D. Fisher 51) drew with Surrey 128 (C.E.W. Silverwood 5–28) and 57–4.

Saturday, September 18. Time to stroll off into the sunset at the end of another season. On the field at least, cricket goes into temporary hibernation before England and England A leave for winter tours. Four of the Yorkshire players, Gough, Hamilton, Vaughan and Silverwood wil be involved. Some members of the playing staff will also be overseas on professional engagements. Others, like Blakey, will find employment here, patiently awaiting the call to arms for pre-season training which will begin in March. Meanwhile, William Hill's are offering odds of 12–1 on Yorkshire to become the winners of County Cricker's inaugural First Division Championship in the year 2000.